T0419643

AGRICULTURE ISSUES AND POLICIES SERIES

# PRICE DYNAMICS BEHIND CONSUMER FOOD PURCHASES

# AGRICULTURE ISSUES AND POLICIES SERIES

**Agriculture Issues & Policies, Volume I**
*Alexander Berk (Editor)*
2001. ISBN: 1-56072-947-3

**Assessing Disease Potential in U.S. Aquaculture Industry**
*Emilija Kalnins (Editor)*
2009. ISBN: 978-1-60741-543-5

**Agricultural Conservation**
*Anthony G. Hargis (Editor)*
2009. ISBN: 978-1-60692-273-6

**Agricultural Conservation**
*Anthony G. Hargis (Editor)*
2009. ISBN: 978-1-60876-813-4
(Online Book)

**Environmental Services and Agriculture**
*Karl T. Poston (Editor)*
2009. ISBN: 978-1-60741-053-9

**Weeds: Management, Economic Impacts and Biology**
*Rudolph V. Kingely (Editor)*
2009. ISBN: 978-1-60741-010-2

**No-Till Farming: Effects on Soil, Pros and Cons and Potential**
*Earl T. Nardali (Editor)*
2009. ISBN: 978-1-60741-402-5

**Inspection and Protection of U.S. Meat and Poultry**
*Finn J. Amundson (Editor)*
2009. ISBN: 978-1-60741-120-8

**Global Beef Trade**
*Alessandro Ferrara (Editor)*
2009. ISBN: 978-1-60741-121-5

**Organic Food - Economics and Issues**
*Earl D. Straub (Editor)*
2009. ISBN: 978-1-60741-130-7

**Soybean and Wheat Crops: Growth, Fertilization and Yield**
*Samuel Davies and George Evans*
2009. ISBN: 978-1-60741-173-4

**Soybean and Wheat Crops: Growth, Fertilization, and Yield**
*Samuel Davies and George Evans*
2009. ISBN: 978-1-61668-984-1
(Online Book)

**Effects of Liberalizing World Agricultural Trade**
*Henrik J. Ehrstrom (Editor)*
2009. ISBN: 978-1-60741-198-7

**Hired Farmworkers: Profile and Labor Issues**
*Rea S. Berube (Editor)*
2009. ISBN: 978-1-60741-232-8

**Effects of Liberalizing World Agricultural Trade**
*Henrik J. Ehrstrom (Editor)*
2009. ISBN: 978-1-60876-601-7
(Online Book)

**Agricultural Wastes**
*Geoffrey S. Ashworth and Pablo Azevedo (Editors)*
2009. ISBN: 978-1-60741-305-9

**Sugar Beet Crops: Growth, Fertilization & Yield**
*Claus T. Hertsburg*
2009. ISBN: 978-1-60741-491-9

**Economic Impacts of Foreign-Source Animal Disease**
*Jace R. Corder (Editor)*
2009. ISBN: 978-1-60741-601-2

**Economic Impacts of Foreign-Source Animal Disease**
*Jace R. Corder (Editor)*
2009. ISBN: 978-1-60876-602-4
(Online Book)

**Essential Oils: Art, Agriculture, Science, Industry and Entrepreneurship(A Focus on the Asia-Pacific Region)**
*Murray Hunter*
2009. ISBN: 978-1-60741-865-8

**America's Family Farms**
*Efren J. Tamayo (Editor)*
2010. ISBN: 978-1-60741-751-4

**Drivers and Restraints for Economically Efficient Farm Production**
*Helena Hansson Karin Larsén Bo Öhlmér*
2009. ISBN: 978-1-60876-171-5

**Corn Crop Production: Growth, Fertilization and Yield**
*Arn T. Danforth*
2009. ISBN: 978-1-60741-955-6

**Corn Crop Production: Growth, Fertilization and Yield**
*Arn T. Danforth*
2009. ISBN: 978-1-60876-860-8
(Online Book)

**Phosphate Solubilizing Microbes for Crop Improvement**
*Mohammad Saghir Khan and Almas Zaidi (Editors)*
2009. ISBN: 978-1-60876-112-8

**Agriculture and Food**
*Claus Schäfer*
2010. ISBN: 978-1-60692-038-1

**Agricultural Economics: New Research**
*Tomas H. Lee (Editor)*
2010. ISBN: 978-1-61668-077-0

**Agricultural Economics: New Research**
*Tomas H. Lee (Editor)*
2010. ISBN: 978-1-61668-445-7
(Online)

**U.S. Biobased Products Market Potential and Projections through 2025**
*Meredith A. Williamson*
2010 ISBN: 978-1-60741-033-1

**The Sugar Industry and Cotton Crops**
*Peter T. Jenkins (Editor)*
2010. ISBN: 978-1-61668-320-7

**The Sugar Industry and Cotton Crops**
*Peter T. Jenkins (Editor)*
2010. ISBN: 978-1-61668-439-6
(Online)

**Tomatoes: Agricultural Procedures, Pathogen Interactions and Health Effects**
*Eric D. Aubé and Frederick H. Poole (Editors)*
2010. ISBN: 978-1-60876-869-1

**Sustainable Agriculture: Technology, Planning and Management**
*Augusto Salazar and Ismael Rios (Editors)*
2010. ISBN: 978-1-60876-269-9

**Organic Farming and Peanut Crops**
*Darren C. Grossman and Terrance L. Barrios (Editors)*
2010. ISBN: 978-1-60876-187-6

**Farm Bill of 2008: Major Provisions and Legislative Action**
*Mary T. Conner (Editor)*
2010. ISBN: 978-1-60741-750-7

**Million Dollar Farms in the New Century**
*Samuel D. Bosworth (Editor)*
2010. ISBN: 978-1-60741-755-2

**Million Dollar Farms an the New Century**
*Samuel D. Bosworth (Editor)*
2010. ISBN: 978-1-61668-541-6
(Online Book)

**Pesticide Resistance, Population Dynamics and Invasive Species Management**
*Gregory J. McKee, Colln A. Carter, James A. Chalfant, Rachael E. Goodhue,and Frank G. Zalom*
2010. ISBN: 978-1-60741-758-3

**Agroforestry Development on the Canadian Prairies**
*Suren N. Kulshreshtha, Ken Van Rees, Hayley Hesseln, Johnston, John Kort*
2010. ISBN: 978-1-61668-266-8

**Agroforestry Development on the Canadian Prairies**
*Suren N. Kulshreshtha, Ken Van Rees, Hayley Hesseln, Johnston, John Kort*
2010. ISBN: 978-1-61668-266-8
(Online Book)

**Agriculture Research and Technology**
*Kristian Bundgaard and Luke Isaksen (Editors)*
2010 ISBN: 978-1-60741-850-4

**Soil Phenols**
*A. Muscolo and M. Sidari (Editors)*
2010. ISBN: 978-1-60876-264-4

**Ecophysiology of Tropical Tree Crops**
*Fabio DeMatta (Editor)*
2010. ISBN: 978-1-60876-392-4

**Agricultural Production**
*Felix C. Wager (Editor)*
2010. ISBN: 978-1-61668-695-6

**Rethinking Structural Reform in Turkish Agriculture: Beyond the World Bank's Strategy**
*Baris Karapinar, Fikret Adaman and Gokhan Ozertan (Editors)*
2010. ISBN: 978-1-60876-718-2

**Manure Use for Fertilizer and Energy**
*Connor D. Macias (Editor)*
2010. ISBN: 978-1-60876-847-9

**Price Dynamics behind Consumer Food Purchases**
*Morgan D. Fitzpatrick (Editor)*
2010. ISBN: 978-1-60876-892-9

**Governance of Agrarian Sustainability**
*Hrabrin Bachev*
2010. ISBN: 978-1-60876-888-2

**Transformation of U.S. Animal Agriculture**
*Justin M. Daigle (Editor)*
2010. ISBN: 978-1-60876-938-4

**The Peanut Plant and Light: Spermidines from Peanut Flowers**
*Victor S. Sobolev, James B. Gloe and Arlene A. Sy*
2010. ISBN: 978-1-61668-028-2

**The Peanut Plant and Light: Spermidines from Peanut Flowers**
*Victor S. Sobolev, James B. Gloer and Arlene A. Sy*
2010. ISBN: 978-1-61668-371-9
(Online Book)

**Agriculture and Environmental Security in Southern Ontario's Watersheds**
*Glen Filson, Bamidele Adekunle, and Katia Marzall*
2010. ISBN: 978-1-61668-156-2

**Agriculture and Environmental Security in Southern Ontario's Watersheds**
*Glen Filson, Bamidele Adekunle and Katia Marzall*
2010. ISBN: 978-1-61668-372-6
(Online Book)

**Alignment-Free Models in Plant Genomics: Theoretical, Experimental, and Legal issues**
*Humberto González-Díaz, Guillermin Agüero-Chapin, Cristian Robert Munteanu, Francisco Prado-Prado, Kuo-Chen Chou, Aliuska Duardo-Sanchez, Grace Patlewicz and Antonio López-Diaz*
2010. ISBN: 978-61668-333-7

**Manure: Management, Uses and Environmental Impacts**
*Carmen S. Dellaguardia (Editor)*
2010. ISBN: 978-1-61668-424-2

**Alignment-Free Models in Plant Genomics: Theoretical, Experimental, and Legal issues**
*Humberto González-Díaz, Guillermin Agüero-Chapin, Cristian Robert Munteanu, Francisco Prado-Prado, Kuo-Chen Chou, Aliuska Duardo-Sanchez, Grace Patlewicz and Antonio López-Diaz*
2010. ISBN: 978-61668-603-1 (Online Book)

**Manure: Management, Uses and Environmental Impacts**
*Carmen S. Dellaguardia (Editor)*
2010. ISBN: 978-1-61668-647-5 (Online Book)

AGRICULTURE ISSUES AND POLICIES SERIES

# PRICE DYNAMICS BEHIND CONSUMER FOOD PURCHASES

MORGAN D. FITZPATRICK
EDITOR

Nova Science Publishers, Inc.
*New York*

For permission to use material from this book please contact us:
Telephone 631-231-7269; Fax 631-231-8175
Web Site: http://www.novapublishers.com



**LIBRARY OF CONGRESS CATALOGING-IN-PUBLICATION DATA**

*Price dynamics behind consumer food purchases / editor, Morgan D. Fitzpatrick.*
*p. cm.*
*Includes index.*
*ISBN 978-1-60876-892-9 (hardcover)*
*1. Food prices. 2. Marketing. I. Fitzpatrick, Morgan D.*
*HD9000.4.P75 2009*
*338.1'9--dc22*
*2009046482*

*Published by Nova Science Publishers, Inc. † New York*

# CONTENTS

# PREFACE

The heightened commodity price volatility of 2008 and the subsequent acceleration in U.S. food price inflation raised concerns and generated many questions about farm and food price movements by members of Congress and their constituents. This book responds to those concerns by addressing the nature and measurement of retail food price inflation. It measures how aggregate food price inflation is measured and compares recent price inflation for both at-home (i.e., retail) purchases and away-from-home consumption, as well as by major food groups. In addition, the major economic concepts underlying consumer food behavior are reviewed. The nature of the statistical indicators used to measure consumer food prices and expenditures are also described. Moreover, this book provides information on recent history and projections for U.S. food expenditure shares relative to total household budget, with comparisons across income quintiles, as well internationally. This book consists of public documents which have been located, gathered, combined, reformatted, and enhanced with a subject index, selectively edited and bound to provide easy access.

Chapter 1 - The heightened commodity price volatility of 2008 and the subsequent acceleration in U.S. food price inflation raised concerns and generated many questions about farm and food price movements by Members of Congress and their constituents. This report responds to those concerns by addressing the nature and measurement of retail food price inflation.

Chapter 2 - The heightened commodity price volatility of 2008 and the subsequent acceleration in U.S. food price inflation have raised concerns and generated many questions about farm and food price movements from Members of Congress and their constituents. This report responds to those concerns by addressing the linkage between farm and retail food prices.

Chapter 3 - Over the past 10 years, the growth of nontraditional retail food outlets has transformed the food market landscape, increasing the variety of shopping and food options available to consumers, as well as price variation in retail food markets. This report focuses on these dynamics and how they affect food price variation across store format types. The differences in prices across store formats are especially noteworthy when compared with standard measures of food price inflation over time. Over the past 20 years, annual food price changes, as measured by the Consumer Price Index (CPI), have averaged just 3 percent per year, while food prices for similar products can vary by more than 10 percent across store formats at any one point in time. Since the current CPI for food does not fully take into account the lower price option of nontraditional retailers, a gap exists between price change as measured using scanner data versus the CPI estimate, even for the relatively low food inflation period of 1998-2003.

In: Price Dynamics Behind Consumer Food... ISBN: 978-1-60876-892-9
Editor: Morgan D. Fitzpatrick 

*Chapter 1*

# CONSUMERS AND FOOD PRICE INFLATION*

***Randy Schnepf[1] and Joe Richardson[2]***
[1]Agricultural Policy
[2]Social Policy

## SUMMARY

The heightened commodity price volatility of 2008 and the subsequent acceleration in U.S. food price inflation raised concerns and generated many questions about farm and food price movements by Members of Congress and their constituents. This report responds to those concerns by addressing the nature and measurement of retail food price inflation.

During the 1991 to 2006 period, U.S. food prices were fairly stable—annual food price inflation, as measured by the U.S. Bureau of Labor Statistics (BLS) Consumer Price Index (CPI) for all food (excluding alcoholic beverages), averaged a relatively low 2.5%. However, several economic factors emerged in late 2005 that began to gradually push market prices higher for both raw agricultural commodities and energy costs, and ultimately retail food prices. U.S. food price inflation increased at a rate of 4% in 2007 and at 5.5% in 2008—the highest since 1990 and well above the general inflation rate of 3.8%.

* This is an edited, reformatted and augmented version of a CRS Report for Congress publication dated June 2009.

By late 2008 the inflationary price trends had reversed. Prices for many raw agricultural commodities had already started to decline by late spring of 2008; however, owing to lags in the adjustment process, it was not until November 2008 that monthly food price inflation fell to near 0%, and it actually declined in February and March 2009. USDA projects that annual food price inflation will ease into a range of 3%-4% in 2009 as lower commodity and energy costs combine with weak domestic and global economies to reduce demand-driven inflation from 2008 levels.

The all-food CPI has two components—food-at-home and food-away-from-home. The food-at-home CPI is most representative of retail food prices and is significantly more volatile than the food-away-from-home index. The food-at-home CPI averaged 6.4% during 2008, compared with a 4.4% annual inflation rate for food-away-from home prices. This difference is partially explained by the larger share of farm products in the final price of retail foods than in food-away-from home. Farm product prices are, in general, substantially more volatile than the other marketing and processing costs that enter into retail or ready-to-eat foods.

Many wages and salaries, as well as federal programs (including several domestic food assistance programs), are linked to price inflation through escalation clauses in order to retain their purchasing power. For households where income and federal benefits do not keep up with price inflation, declines in purchasing power are real and immediate. However, even for households with escalation clauses, a time lag usually occurs between the time the price inflation is measured and the time when the wage or program benefit is adjusted upward to compensate.

The 2008-2009 global economic crisis—which encompasses higher retail prices, unemployment, income loss, and lower effective household purchasing power—has manifested itself in higher participation rates in the federal Supplemental Nutrition Assistance Program (SNAP), formerly known as the Food Stamp Program. As of March 2009, participation in the SNAP was at an all- time high of 33.2 million persons (or one in every 10 Americans). Other domestic food assistance programs also have seen increased participation and costs. In response to advocates' calls for increased federal assistance, Congress approved (in February 2009) additional support for domestic food assistance programs totaling $20.8 billion over 10 years via the stimulus package (the American Recovery and Reinvestment Act of 2009; P.L. 111-5).

# INTRODUCTION

Everyone eats. As a result, everyone is affected to some degree by food price changes. This makes understanding food price changes and their effects on consumers an important matter for Congress. This report provides information on measuring food price changes and how such changes relate to U.S. consumers.

The first section of the report, "Consumer Demand," briefly reviews the major economic concepts underlying consumer food behavior. The second section, "Major Statistical Indicators of Consumer Expenditures and Food Price Changes," describes the nature of the statistical indicators used to measure consumer food prices and expenditures. It includes a subsection, "Historic Price Inflation Patterns," describing how U.S. food price inflation rates have evolved since 1915, when federal price data collection for inflation measuring purposes began. The third section, "Consumer Income and Expenditures," provides information on recent history and projections for U.S. food expenditure shares relative to total household budget, with comparisons across income quintiles, as well as internationally. The fourth section, "Recent Food Price Inflation," examines retail food price inflation, including a review and discussion of the level of food price inflation registered by the consumer price index for all-food, at-home, and away-fromhome food purchases as well as for major food groups. Finally, in the section entitled "Effect of High Prices," the report discusses the impact that rapid food price inflation can have on government food programs and the more vulnerable consumer groups.

Each section may be read independently of the others. Thus, those readers that are concerned primarily with the status of U.S. food price inflation may proceed directly to the sections entitled "Historic Price Inflation Patterns" or "Recent Food Price Inflation."

# CONSUMER DEMAND

Consumer demand is influenced by economic factors—own-price, the price of close substitutes, the price of complementary items, and household income—as well as by several non-economic factors including tastes and preferences, family size, age of family members, geographic location, shopping behavior, and lifestyle choices. Economists attempt to study and measure the nature of consumer behavior in response to changes in prices, incomes, and household characteristics, with an eye for understanding the potential social welfare outcomes that may result from price and income changes across different socioeconomic groups. Policymakers, in turn, often attempt to use that information to design and implement policies that mitigate the more deleterious effects of price and income changes on consumers.

## Price Responsiveness

In general, consumers will use less of any good if its price increases relative to other goods (referred to as the pure "substitution effect" by economists). However, a consumer's price responsiveness is a matter of degree and is subject to the potential influence of disposable income as well as other non-price factors such as those listed in the preceding paragraph.

Under most circumstances, the availability of many close substitutes is likely to make consumers more sensitive or responsive to price changes, because they have the opportunity to switch to similar alternatives. In contrast, a lack of substitutes may give the consumer little choice but to continue to purchase the available good, even as its price rises, especially if it is deemed a necessity. Strong ethnic or cultural tastes and preferences may endear a person to a particular food type such that he or she will continue to purchase that food as its price rises even in the presence of abundant substitutes (for example, ethnic groups that are accustomed to eating rice at every meal may be reluctant to switch to bread or potatoes even if the price of rice rises relative to those other foods).

Rapid or unexpected changes in retail food prices will impact some consumers more than others depending on income levels and the importance of the affected food items in consumers' budgets. In general, if an item represents a very small portion of the consumer's budget (for example, consider salt), then a consumer is less likely to respond to a price change. Basic food staples such as bread, potatoes, pasta, and rice tend to take smaller shares of the consumer's food budget (relative to meat, dairy products, fruits and vegetables, and more processed food products) and, as a result, consumers are less responsive to a change in their price. In contrast, high-valued food items such as expensive cuts of meat or seafood probably represent more costly (and infrequently purchased) delicacies for most households. As a result, most households will tend to be far more responsive to changes in the prices of such high-valued products than for basic staples. Often a price change for an item within a specific food group[1] may result in consumers switching to lower-quality items within that food category—the classic example being a switch from steak to hamburger when meat prices rise. In contrast, a widespread price rise across all food groups may engender substantial reshuffling of consumer food budget allocations as households try to meet their nutritional goals with their limited budgets.

Of course, the absolute size of a consumer's disposable income is also important in determining actual purchasing power. For households with smaller incomes, the food budget itself is likely a larger portion of total household expenditures, and such households are likely to be more responsive to price changes across all food categories than are higher-income households.

In summary, lower-income consumers who spend a significant share of their household budget on food are likely to be impacted more severely by rising food prices (and are likely to be more responsive to price changes) than high-income consumers with lower food budget shares.

## Income Responsiveness

A household's absolute level of disposable income (and, to a lesser degree, wealth) directly affects its ability to respond to price changes. As a result, as household incomes grow, consumers often opt for more expensive or higher-quality selections of foods than are presently in their food budget, or may experiment by trying new or unfamiliar foods. For example, as incomes increase in less-developed countries, it is common to see per-capita expenditures on meat and dairy products increase. In contrast, when incomes decline, consumers tend to pull back from more expensive options. If the income decline is severe and is perceived as permanent or long-lasting, consumers may make substantial changes to their food budget choices.

In the aggregate, household consumption behavior in response to perceived income changes (if persistent and widespread) may affect a country's agricultural production or trade patterns. As a result, it is important for policymakers to monitor household wealth and income levels and distribution for unexpected shifts that may have important economic consequences.

Economists call the relationship between changes in consumer income and the quantity of an item purchased an *Engel curve*. This relationship is used by economists to classify goods.

- For a **normal good,** consumers buy more of it as their incomes increase, but at a decreasing rate such that its average budget share declines for higher income levels.
- For a **luxury good**, consumers buy more of it as their incomes increase and at an increasing rate such that its budget share increases at higher income levels.
- For an **inferior good,** consumers buy less of it as their incomes increase.

Of course, different goods will be classified differently by different people since tastes and preferences also are important. However, with respect to the overall food budget, in the aggregate certain behavioral norms are expected. *Engel 's law* is the idea (largely validated by data with some minor exceptions) that food, in general, is a normal good, so that the budget share spent on food declines as a consumer's income rises. While Engel's law is generally observable for individual households, it tends to hold best in the aggregate—that is, when considering an entire population. To the extent that this "law" holds, then the proportion of a nation's income spent on food serves as a good index for international comparisons of relative consumer welfare.

## Tastes and Preferences

Non-economic factors such as cultural or ethnic preferences may determine both the share of a particular food product in the household's budget (e.g., rice represents a larger share of per-capita expenditure in most Asian households than in most European households at similar income levels) as well as a household's responsiveness to a change in the price of a particular product.

Dietary needs also change with age. For example, young children and adolescents generally need both more calories and a higher portion of protein-based calories to meet nutritional demands of rapid physical growth and high activity levels. Populations or households with a large share of individuals from this demographic stratum are more likely to consume larger per-capita portions of meat and dairy products than an older, more mature and sedentary population would. As a result, population demographics such as household composition, size, and age structure often play an important role in consumer price sensitivity and income responsiveness. In increasingly affluent societies, lifestyle choices, when complemented with sufficient purchasing power, can also play an influential role in household food purchases.

### Summary

For households with low disposable income levels where food expenditures are a large share of the budget, rising food prices result in greater responsiveness and may force more difficult budgetary tradeoffs than in higher-income households with smaller food-budget shares. Of course the opposite effect is true during periods of falling prices. However, each household's price and income effects also are influenced by its particular set of non-economic characteristics.

## MAJOR STATISTICAL INDICATORS OF CONSUMER EXPENDITURES AND FOOD PRICE CHANGES

Several government agencies produce useful statistical indicators for measuring and monitoring consumer expenditure behavior and food prices in the United States. The monthly Consumer Price Index (CPI) produced by the Department of Labor's Bureau of Labor Statistics (BLS) is the most widely recognized indicator of consumer price inflation. It is described in detail below along with a brief discussion of the Personal Consumption Expenditure (PCE) price deflator prepared by the Department of Commerce's Bureau of Economic Analysis (BEA).[2]

In contrast to the CPI, which is largely unique as a statistical indicator of consumer price changes, several different indicators of both consumer income and food expenditures are available, due primarily to important differences in how food expenditures and personal income are defined by the different data series. As a result, each of these data sources has certain strengths and weaknesses depending on how it is to be used.

The BLS, in addition to producing the CPI, is also responsible for producing and reporting on the annual Consumer Expenditure Survey (CES). The CES is the only federal survey that allows users to associate the complete range of household expenditures with the major characteristics and incomes of those households. The CES is discussed in more detail below.

Two alternate sources of information on personal income are produced by the Department of Commerce's U.S. Census Bureau and the BEA.[3] The Census Bureau collects data and reports annually on both household income and characteristics.[4] However, Census income data do not include information on household expenditures.

The BEA produces a set of national income and product accounts (NIPAs) that provide information on the value and composition of output produced in the United States by major sector during a given period, and on the distribution and uses of the income generated by that output.[5] The BEA complements the aggregate NIPA data with population estimates from the Census Bureau to derive per-capita estimates of personal income and outlays by major category. However, NIPA data are aggregate national account indicators, not household indicators.

The U.S. Department of Agriculture's Economic Research Service (ERS) combines data from the above sources with other information to conduct economic analyses across a range of consumer food price and expenditure topics.[6] Four noteworthy research products include:

- **Food CPI Forecasts**—short-term (12- to 18-month) forecasts of U.S. food price inflation for all food, food-away-from home, and food-at-home, with the latter category broken out into 15 selected food subcategories.[7]

- **Food Expenditure Tables**—aggregate food expenditure estimates produced from national data that measure current sales or receipts by each type of store that sells food.[8] ERS methods provide a comprehensive measure of the total value of all food expenditures by all final purchasers including government agencies, businesses, and nonprofit organizations.

- **Food Baseline Projections**—projections for the U.S. agricultural sector 10 years ahead, including crop production, agricultural trade, farm income, and consumer food prices and expenditures.[9] Projections are a description of what would be expected to happen under the 2008 farm bill (P.L. 110-246), with very specific external circumstances.

- **Price and Income Response Elasticities**—detailed estimates of consumer price and income responsiveness, and food expenditure behavior, across different income groupings both within the United States[10] and for low-, middle-, and high-income countries.[11]

## Consumer Expenditure Survey (CES)

The CES is a nationwide, annual household survey that collects information on expenditures for goods (including food items) and services used in day-to-day living.[12] In addition, the CES collects information on household income and household characteristics such as the number, age, race, education, and gender of household members, housing tenure status, and household assets and liabilities.

The CES is designed to represent the total U.S. civilian non-institutional population. It has been collected annually by the U.S. Census Bureau—under contract with BLS—since 1979.[13] Prior to 1979, the CES was conducted every 10 to 12 years.

The CES uses two main survey components, an interview and a diary, to collect information.

- The **interview survey** is designed to obtain data on the types of expenditures respondents can recall for a period of three months or longer. In general, these are relatively large expenditures such as those for property, automobiles, or major appliances, or they occur on a regular basis such as rent, utilities, or insurance premiums. Approximately 14,000 addresses are contacted each calendar quarter of each year. Usable interview data is obtained from approximately 7,100 households each quarter.
- The **diary survey** is designed to obtain expenditure data on small, frequently purchased items such as food and beverage expenditures (both at home and in eating places), housekeeping supplies and services, nonprescription drugs, and personal care products. About 12,000 addresses are selected each year to complete a diary survey of household expenditures for two consecutive one-week periods. Usable diary data is obtained from approximately 7,100 households.

### *Major Uses of CES Data*

An important use of CES data is for periodic updating of the Consumer Price Index (CPI) market basket of goods and services, as well as to determine the relative importance of CPI components and to derive new cost weights for the market basket items.[14]

Another important use of CES data is to allow data users to relate the expenditures and income of consumers to key characteristics of those consumers. For example, CES data are used by both government and private agencies to study the welfare of different segments of the population such as the elderly, low-income families, urban families, and those receiving food stamps. CES data are used by policymakers to evaluate the potential effects of policy changes on levels of living among diverse socioeconomic groups. Also, market researchers may use CES data to analyze the demand for various goods and services by different demographic groups. Because of the large survey sample size and the representative nature of sample selection, the CES data also allow for regional comparisons.

### *Household-Level Expenditures versus National Average Disposable Income*

Clearly, only the CES household-level data allow analysts to evaluate food expenditure behavior while controlling for specific household characteristics. However, ERS has shown (as discussed below) that national accounts data can provide a more comprehensive evaluation of national food expenditure behavior by capturing food industry and other non-household food behavior that is otherwise omitted from a household survey. These differences are briefly discussed here.

## National Accounts Data: Focus on Food Expenditure Trends

For monitoring national food expenditure trends and patterns (e.g., food budget shares or food-at-home versus away-from-home consumption patterns) food expenditure estimates based on aggregate account data generally provide the most useful information. In this regard, the ERS food expenditure series is perhaps the most qualified and easily accessible of available data series. ERS uses primarily Census Bureau data (as classified under the North American Industry classification System (NAICS)) to construct very detailed and comprehensive food expenditure series based on specific industry and business food sales.[15]

Unlike NIPAs, ERS food expenditure calculations exclude pet food, ice, and prepared animal feeds, as well as nonfoods such as drugs and branded supplies, in estimating at-home food purchases.

Unlike CES data, ERS food expenditure estimates include non-household purchases and acquisitions—for example, government food purchases for domestic military personnel, the value of school meals (including "free lunches" distributed under the National School Lunch Program), and the value of food purchased by airlines for serving during flights.

**CES Household Data: Focus on Individual Consumer Behavior**

For evaluating household purchases and consumer behavior, household-level expenditure data (as available from the CES) are generally preferable to aggregate income measures such as the disposable personal income (DPI) data available from either the Census or the BEA. There are two primary reasons for this. First, the CES expenditure data are collected at the household level, thus permitting household comparisons rather than relying on the national averages available from the NIPA data. Second, household expenditures are generally more stable than household income measures—even during periods of unemployment by household members, the household will continue to make purchases of routine items such as food. Thus, household expenditure data are less subject to the gyrations of the general economy.

Household expenditure data can be more reliably measured by survey data than can household income data. As a matter of fact, it is not uncommon for CES data for household annual expenditures to exceed reported income before taxes, particularly for households from lower- income groups. Why? Some CES interview respondents may be reluctant to answer inquiries concerning their income. Some households whose members may experience a spell of unemployment may draw on their savings to maintain their expenditures. Self-employed consumers may experience business losses that result in low or even negative incomes for a period, but are able to maintain their expenditures by borrowing or relying on savings. Students may get by on loans while they are in school, and retirees may rely on savings and investments.

## Consumer Price Index (CPI)

The CPI is perhaps the most widely reported measure of U.S. price inflation.[16] The CPI is a composite measure of the average change over time in the prices paid by U.S. urban consumers for a defined market basket of goods (including food) and services that people buy for day-to-day living.[17] Since its focus is on consumer expenditures, it intentionally excludes government expenditures and the cost of inputs used by manufacturing and agriculture. The CPI is used both as an economic indicator of retail price inflation and as a means of adjusting current-period values for inflation.

### *Is the CPI's Food Market Basket Representative?*[18]

The BLS is responsible for collecting monthly price data for the market basket of consumer expenditure categories from across the United States, then calculating and reporting the monthly price indexes (or CPIs) for those items. The mix of goods and services making up the market basket is based on spending patterns established by the annual CES, and is updated every two years. The prices of market basket items are drawn from representative urban settings across the United States. According to BLS, the consumer groups included in the sample pool (referred to as the U-population and used to create the CPI-U index) represent 87% of the total U.S. population including professionals, the self-employed, the poor, the unemployed, and retired people.[19] Not included in the CPI are spending patterns of people living in rural non-metropolitan areas, farm families, people in the Armed Forces, and those in institutions.

### *CPI Categories and Weights*

The BLS collects prices each month in 87 urban areas across the United States for about 80,000 items from approximately 23,000 retail establishments (including department stores, filling stations, supermarkets, hospitals, etc.).[20] All taxes directly associated with the purchase and use of items are included in the index. The data are further combined, based on population size, into 38 different urban geographic areas.[21] The data on goods and services are aggregated into 211 categories. As a result, basic price indexes are available for 38 x 211 = 8,018 area-item combinations. Higher-level indexes are produced by calculating a weighted average across the relevant basic indexes. The weights are derived from reported expenditures from the CES. BLS updates the expenditure weights every two years.

The "All-Items" CPI is the index most often referred to (i.e., the headline CPI) for representing consumer price inflation, and represents a weighted index based on the indexes from all areas and for all categories of goods and services whose prices are collected. The all-items CPI is generally divided into eight major spending categories, including a "Food and Beverage" category (Figure 1), which accounts for 15.8% of average consumer expenditures. This compares with the Housing category's dominant share of 43.4% of annual consumer expenditures and the Transportation category's 15.3% share.[22]

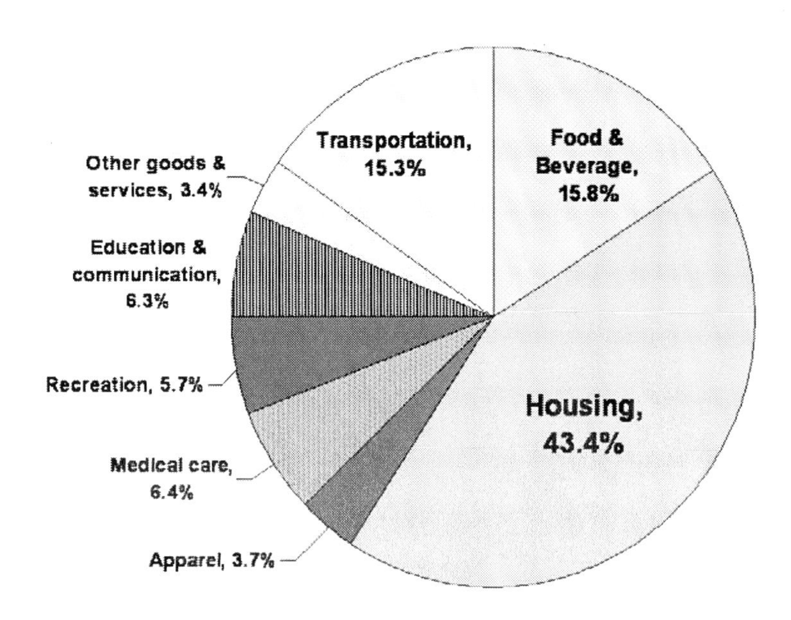


Source: U.S. Department of Labor, BLS.
Note: As of December 2008 (based on the 2005-06 CES).

Figure 1. CPI Relative Weights by Major Category.

The CPI category of "Food and Beverages" is composed of two major subcategories: "All-Food" (which has a relative weight of 14.6% in the all-items CPI), and "Alcoholic Beverages" (1.1%). The all-food CPI is the principal indicator of consumer food price changes. The all-food CPI can be subdivided into the "Food-at-Home" and "Food-Away-from-Home" categories. The **food-at-home CPI** reflects changes in the prices of foods consumed at home. As such it is the principal indicator of changes in retail food prices in the United States. The **food-away-from-home CPI** reflects changes in the prices of foods purchased outside of the home, primarily at eating and drinking places such as restaurants and other eating establishments. However, it also includes price changes for ready-to-eat foods purchased at hotels and motels, recreational places and sporting events, vending machines, and school and work cafeterias.

***Historic Price Inflation Patterns***

Over time, the all-food and all-items CPIs have moved together, although the all-food CPI has been consistently more variable than the all-items CPI (**Figure 2** and **Table 1**). Prior to 1960, both of these indexes exhibited higher average inflation rates and more volatility than in recent years. During the 19 14-1920 period, both price indexes recorded double-digit annual inflation. Food inflation hit its all-time high of 28.7% in 1917 (**Figure 2**). All-items price inflation peaked a year later at 18%. Just four years later retail prices entered a prolonged deflationary period, starting in 1921 with a deflationary plunge of -24.2% for all-food and -10.5% for all-items, that lasted until 1941 when war time shortages finally renewed retail price inflation.

The variability of the overall CPI and its individual components is important because uncertainty about price changes makes planning more difficult—whether it is the investment planning of a business, the meal planning of a household, or the policy intervention planning of a government agency.

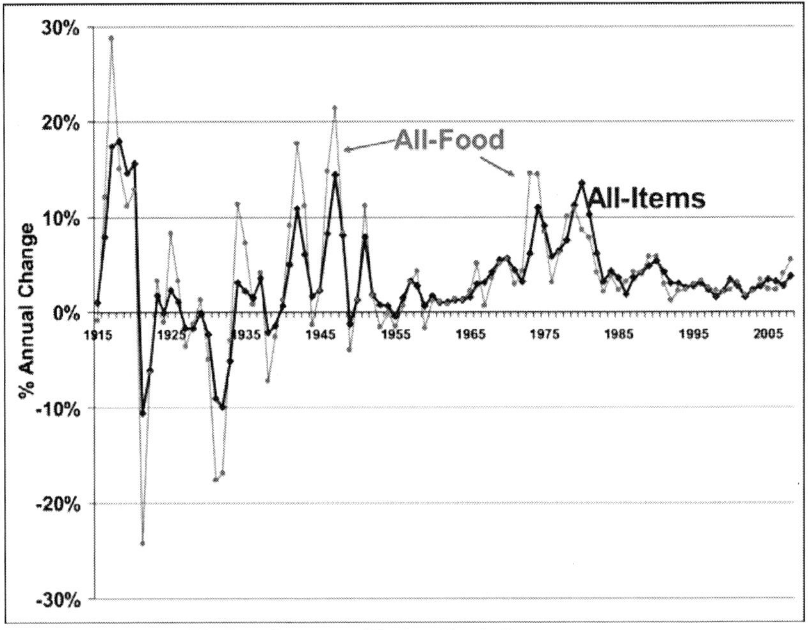


Source: Department of Labor, Bureau of Labor Statistics.

Notes: The percent change is calculated from the annual average CPI for successive years.

Figure 2. Annual Price Inflation, 1915-2008: All-Items vs. All-Food.

**Table 1. Retail Price Change, Mean and Variability, by Historic Time Period (All Data—Mean and Standard Deviation (SD)—Are Percentages)**

| CPI Series | 1914-1920 | | 1921-1941 | | 1941-1960 | | 1960-1983 | | 1983-2008 | |
|---|---|---|---|---|---|---|---|---|---|---|
| | Mean | SD | Mean | SD | Mean | SD | Mean | SD | Mean | SD |
| **All-Items** | **10.8** | **7.4** | **-1.4** | **4.5** | **3.9** | **4.1** | **5.3** | **3.6** | **3.1** | **0.9** |
| Energy | — | — | — | — | — | — | 6.9 | 9.1 | 3.6 | 7.1 |
| **All-Food** | **11.6** | **9.6** | **- 1.8** | **9.0** | **4.9** | **7.2** | **5.2** | **4.1** | **3.1** | **1.2** |
| At-Home | — | — | — | — | — | — | 5.0 | 4.5 | 3.1 | 1.6 |
| Away-from-Home | — | — | — | — | — | — | 6.0 | 3.1 | 3.2 | 0.9 |
| **Core**[a] | — | — | — | — | — | — | **5.1** | **3.3** | **3.2** | **1.1** |

Source: Calculations were made by CRS based on BLS CPI data.

Notes: "—" = not available. The mean is the average annual price change for each period. The standard deviation (SD) is a measure of dispersion around the mean value for each period. Plus or minus one (two) SD captures 68.2% (95.4%) of the variation around the mean value for each period. The mean and SD have been calculated using the annual percent change data for each of the five different periods. A larger SD implies greater variability, for example, all-food price inflation has shown a clear pattern of declining variability as the SD has fallen from 9.6% during the 1914-20 period to 4.1% during 1960-83 (more than halving the variability), and finally to 1.2% during 1983-2008 (a further decline of over 70% in variability).

a. The "Core" price index is the all-items CPI without the energy and all-food components.

During the 1941-1960 period, price inflation remained extremely volatile, alternating between spikes of inflation and steep disinflationary (i.e., deflationary) drops. It was not until 1960 that retail prices stabilized with tolerably mild inflation. However, this proved short-lived as the 1970s saw a return to sharp price spikes generated by an energy crisis and rapid, unexpected shifts in global crop supply and demand.[23] By the early 1980s, retail price inflation had returned to modest levels below 5%. Since 1983 retail prices, as measured by the all-items and the all-food CPIs, have been relatively low and relatively stable, except for temporary surges in 1989-1990 and again in 2007-2008.

***Overall Inflation versus Core Inflation***

Many economists and policymakers believe that the food and energy components of the CPI are volatile and subject to shocks not easily dealt with through government monetary policy. In response, the BLS also reports another price index, referred to as the “core” index because it removes the food and energy price components from the all-items CPI.[24] The so-called core CPI is thought to be a useful measure of underlying trend inflation in the short run. According to BLS data, the food component of the CPI, although more volatile than the overall CPI, is still substantially less volatile than the energy component (**Figure 3** and **Table 1**).

Since 1960, the energy price index has been a more volatile component of the all-items CPI than the food price index by a substantial margin. For example, the energy price inflation standard deviation (SD) of 9.1% was more than double the all-food SD of 4.1% during the 1960-1983 period, and nearly six times larger since 1983 (7.1% versus 1.2%).

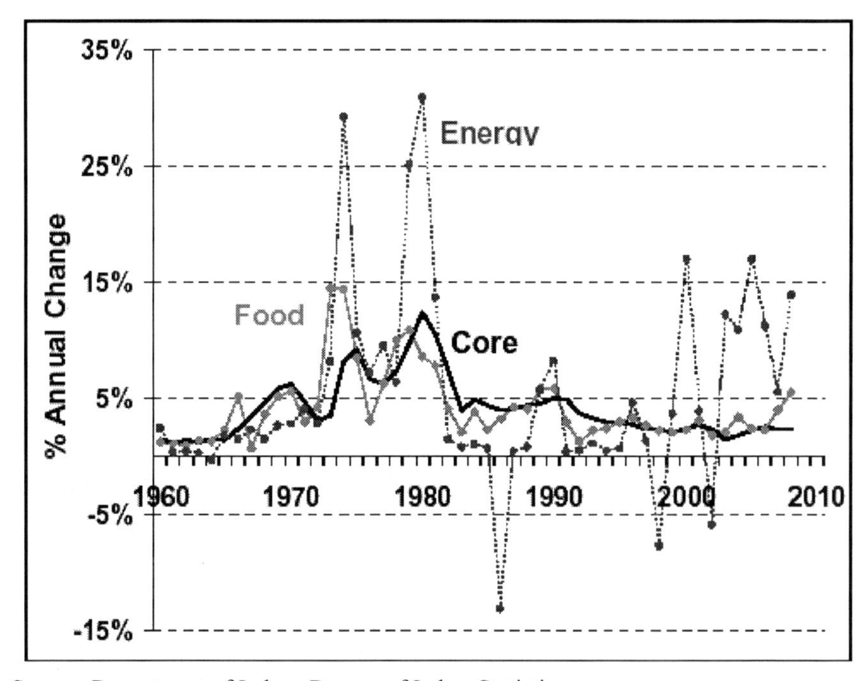


Source: Department of Labor, Bureau of Labor Statistics.

Figure 3. Annual Price Inflation Since 1960: All-Items, All-Food, and Energy.

Since 1983 both the all-food and the all-items CPIs have been lower (in terms of average values) and substantially more stable (in terms of SDs) than during the preceding seven decades. In contrast, the energy price index has been substantially more volatile since 1983 (although at a lower mean level) than it was during the preceding two decades. This is an important point because the energy price index has seen its weighted share of the CPI gradually increase over time and, although energy's current weight share of 7.6% is only about half that of the food weight share of 14.6%, energy price inflation is far more insidious than food inflation to the extent that energy costs figure in the retail price of practically every other component of the CPI.

### *What about Seasonality Patterns in the Data?*

Some monthly price data are subject to seasonal influences that normally occur at the same time and in about the same magnitude every year, independent of market phenomena or consumer income shifts, or household characteristics. For example, meat purchases generally increase in the summer months, when the "grilling" season is open. As a result, the meat market experiences a general surge in demand during the summer months that is independent of incomes, household characteristics, or other economic or demographic factors.

For most price indexes, BLS reports two series—a seasonally adjusted index that removes systematic seasonal influences from the data, and the original unadjusted data.[25] The seasonally adjusted data, including the all-items index levels, are subject to revision for up to five years after their original release. In contrast, the unadjusted data are not subject to revision, even when the index formula is itself altered. This is because many wage contracts and government program benefits are indexed via an escalation agreement to the unadjusted CPI. A revision of historical CPI data would necessarily imply a revision of all wage and benefit payments made under the previously unrevised CPI series.

For analyzing general price trends in the economy, the BLS recommends using seasonally adjusted price indexes since they eliminate price movements that result from seasonal phenomena such as changing climatic conditions, production cycles, model changeovers, holidays, and sales. In contrast, BLS recommends using unadjusted price indexes when the primary interest to consumers is the price actually paid. Unadjusted price indexes are used extensively for escalation purposes in collective bargaining agreements or pension plans.[26]

***Is the Food-at-Home CPI a Good Measure of Retail Food Price Change?***

As mentioned above, the food-at-home CPI is the principal indicator of changes in retail food prices in the United States. Because of its central role as a measure of retail food price inflation, the food-at-home CPI is routinely subject to public scrutiny by food market participants including industry groups, consumer and hunger advocacy groups, and policymakers. A chief concern is whether and to what extent there are any persistent biases in the food-at-home CPI. If the CPI's market basket of items and their respective weights fail to adjust in step with consumer expenditure behavior or if the method for calculating price changes is itself faulty, then the process would likely produce a biased statistical measure of price change.

Indeed, research by BLS and ERS analysts suggests that the food-at-home CPI has tended to overstate retail food price inflation. In particular, they identified four specific problems in the CPI's construction that have imparted an upward bias in the food-at-home CPI.[27]

1. Consumers' spending patterns change, albeit gradually, over time. For example, an aging population (as in the United States) tends to consume less meat and alcohol, but larger shares of cereals and bakery products. Also, food budget shares have declined over time with rising incomes, and an increasing share of food spending has gone for away-from-home consumption.
2. Prices for some food items—particularly fresh fruits and vegetables and fresh meats—may vary widely on occasion. If not accounted for, these fluctuations create an inflationary drift by attaching greater weight to price increases than to decreases. For example, a $0.50 increase on a $1.00 price is a 50% increase, whereas a return to the $1.00 from the $1.50 price is only a 33% price decrease.
3. Price indexes must keep up with the introduction of new food items and new stores to fully represent consumer price alternatives. For example, the CPI has been slow to incorporate the rapid expansion of discount stores that often sell food items at substantially lower prices than traditional grocery stores.[28]
4. Fixed-weight price indexes are vulnerable to a substitution bias.[29] A fixed-weight index does not allow for the likelihood that consumers respond to relative price changes by changing the quantity or quality of their food purchases. For example, price rises due to higher quality

should not count as inflation, since the consumer is getting more product value for the higher price.

BLS has responded to these problems over time by implementing a series of changes to its methods for incorporating and weighting price information from new stores and for new products starting in 1981. In addition, starting in 2002, BLS began updating the expenditure weight shares every 2 years. Prior to 2002, such revisions were more episodic, occurring every 10 to 12 years. A continual rebalancing of the market basket to include new products and more current expenditure weights helps to ensure that the CPI more accurately reflects how consumers allocate their spending.

BLS also has introduced new methods of index construction (in particular, a geometric mean formula for within-item averages) to minimize problems associated with sharply fluctuating prices and possible inflationary drift. However, this adaptation does not capture substitution across items, only within items (thus mitigating lower-level substitution bias). In other words, it would not capture a price-related shift from steak to hamburger, only a shift between differently priced steaks. BLS began to publish a new chained index (the C-CPI-U) in August 2002, to more closely approximate the substitution across expenditure categories that consumers undertake when relative prices change.[30] However, the traditional all-items CPI (CPI-U) remains the most widely quoted price index and still is subject to the higher-level substitution bias.

### *Why Not Use the PCE Price Index to Measure Consumer Price Inflation?*

An alternate measure of inflation—the Personal Consumption Expenditure (PCE) price index—is produced by the Department of Commerce's Bureau of Economic Analysis (BEA).[31] The PCE price index measures the change in prices paid for goods and services by the personal sector in the U.S. national income and product accounts (NIPAs).

Despite their apparent similarity, the CPI and PCE price indexes are constructed differently, they behave differently over time, and they have different purposes and uses.[32] The PCE price index is based on national accounts data and is primarily used for macroeconomic analysis and forecasting. In contrast, the CPI is based on household survey data and measures the change in prices paid by urban consumers for a market basket of consumer goods and services; it is primarily used as an economic indicator and as a means of adjusting current-period data for inflation. Because of this later use, historical CPI data are never revised (unlike PCE data).

Analysts at BEA and BLS have identified four major differences between the CPI and the PCE price indexes. First, they are calculated using different formulas.[33] Second, each formula's set of weights is different (the CPI uses base-year weights versus the PCE's current-year weights). Third, the CPI measures "out-of-pocket" expenditures based on individual household survey data, whereas the PCE price index measures the aggregate outlay for all goods and services purchased by households and nonprofit institutions as drawn from national accounts. Finally, the BEA and BLS analysts cite an accumulation of other minor differences in seasonality adjustments, pricing, and a residual difference due to the underlying data used for each index.

Empirical tests conducted by BEA and BLS analysts suggest that differences in the formulas and the weights account for most of the difference in how the two indexes measure inflation. The CPI uses a formula whereby the weights for goods and services are determined by household expenditures in the base year. In successive years, the same fixed "base" of weighted goods and services is valued using the new year's prices. A shortcoming of this approach is that, because the weights for individual goods and services are fixed, consumer substitution due to relative price changes is not captured by the index. In contrast, the PCE price index uses current-year expenditures to determine the weights. As a result, the PCE price index fully captures consumer substitution among detailed items as the relative price of those items changes.

However, PCE price index methodology is difficult, if not entirely impractical, to implement using household expenditure data. Household survey data are available with a substantial lag due to collection and preparation time, and thus are generally not available for the most current period. This precludes calculating current-year weights as per the PCE formula. As a result, the CPI's base-year weighting appears to be the most timely and practical (although perhaps not the most theoretically sound) method for calculating a price index.

## CONSUMER INCOME AND EXPENDITURES

A household allocates its available income across a range of expenditure, savings, and investment choices. As mentioned earlier, food expenditures as a share of a household's total budget are an indicator of sensitivity (or vulnerability) to unexpected food price changes. At the national level, food budget share (via Engel's law) can be used as a general indicator of welfare among nations.

## Food as a Share of Consumer's Budget

According to Bureau of Economic Analysis (BEA) estimates, in 2007 total U.S. disposable personal income (DPI) was $10,171 billion, or $33,707 per capita.[34] Of these estimates, ERS calculates that, on average, 9.8% of disposable personal income was spent on food.[35]

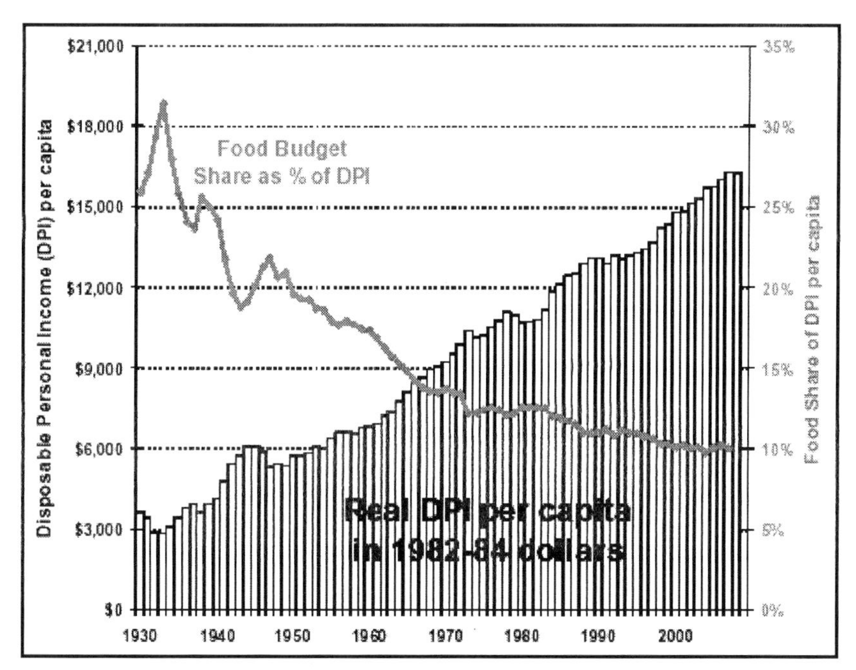


Source: "Food CPI, Prices and Expenditures Briefing Room," Food Expenditure Tables, ERS, USDA.

Notes: Real DPI is BEA nominal DPI series deflated by the all-items CPI with base 1982-1984 = 100; real food expenditures are the ERS series of food expenditures deflated by the all-food CPI with base 1982-1984 = 100.

Figure 4. Comparison of Real U.S. Disposable Personal Income (DPI) Per Capita and the Share of DPI Spent on Food, 1930-2007.

**Figure 4** shows the evolution of the average food budget share against U.S. DPI per capita in constant 1982-1984 average dollars. By both measures (food budget share and real DPI per capita), U.S. consumers have seen their "well-being" improve substantially over the past 70 years. (Note that these are national averages that ignore any potential distribution issues.) The U.S. food share of real DPI has fallen from a high of 31.4% in 1933 to about 10% since 2000, while the average DPI per capita (in 1982-1984 dollars) has risen from $2,824 in 1933 to over $16,000 by 2006.

When measured as a share of average total consumer expenditures of $49,638 per household (based on Consumer Expenditure Survey (CES) data, **Table 2**), average food outlays of $6,133 per household accounted for 12.4% of total spending in 2007.[36] As mentioned earlier, the difference between the two estimates of food budget share (9.8% based on DPI versus 12.4% based on CES total expenditures) is due to how disposable income and food expenditures are calculated for each of these indicators.

**Table 2. Average Household Food Expenditures in 2007 by Income Quintiles**

| Income Quintile | Total | All Food | Food-at-Home | Food-Away-from-Home |
|---|---|---|---|---|
| **Expenditures per household** | | | | |
| Highest 20% | $96,752 | $10,444 | $5,265 | $5,179 |
| Fourth 20% | $57,285 | $7,242 | $3,980 | $3,262 |
| Third 20% | $42,447 | $5,682 | $3,333 | $2,349 |
| Second 20% | $31,150 | $4,260 | $2,741 | $1,519 |
| Lowest 20% | $20,471 | $3,035 | $2,005 | $1,030 |
| **Average Outlay ($)** | **$49,638** | **$6,133** | **$3,465** | **$2,668** |
| **Share of Expenditures: Total and (All Food)** | | | | |
| Highest 20% | 100% | 10.8% (100%) | 5.4% (50.4%) | 5.4% (49.6%) |
| Fourth 20% | 100% | 12.6% (100%) | 6.9% (55.0%) | 5.7% (45.0%) |
| Third 20% | 100% | 13.4% (100%) | 7.9% (58.7%) | 5.5% (41.3%) |
| Second 20% | 100% | 13.7% (100%) | 8.8% (64.3%) | 4.9% (35.7%) |
| Lowest 20% | 100% | 14.8% (100%) | 9.8% (66.1%) | 5.0% (33.9%) |
| **Average Outlay (%)** | **100%** | **12.4% (100%)** | **7.0% (56.5%)** | **5.4% (43.5%)** |

Source: Table 1. Quintiles of before-tax income: Average annual expenditures and characteristics, Consumer Expenditure Survey, 2007, BLS, Dept. of Labor, at http://www.bls.gov/cex/2007/Standard/quintile.pdf.

The estimated food share of household expenditures (**Table 2**) varied across income quintiles in the United States, in accordance with Engel's law—that is, each succeeding higher income quintile increased its absolute expenditures on food (in dollar terms), but at a decreasing rate such that the food budget share declines across higher quintiles. For example, the lowest 20% of U.S. households spent $3,035 on food, or 14.8% of their average total expenditures of $20,471 in 2007. The budget food outlay increases in absolute dollars, while the food budget share declines across income quintiles until the wealthiest quintile, where households spent an average of $10,444 on food, or 10.8% of their total budget of $96,752.

Another clear pattern that emerges from the CES data (**Table 2**) is the propensity to spend more of the food budget on away-from-home food consumption at higher income levels, both in absolute dollars and as a share of the food budget (refer to the percentages in parentheses in **Table 2**). Or, otherwise stated, lower-income U.S. households tend to spend a larger share of their food budget on at-home consumption and are thus more vulnerable to unexpected retail food price increases (this is discussed further in the next section).

## At-Home versus Away-from-Home Consumption

U.S. households have shown a strong propensity over time to increase their share of annual food consumption outside of the home (**Figure 5**). This tendency is associated with increasing per-capita disposable income as mentioned above. It is also associated with increasing female participation in the labor force, more two-earner households, increased advertising and promotion by large food-service chains, increasing time constraints on household members (e.g., longer commutes, increased work hours and less leisure time, etc.), the smaller size of U.S. households, and the increased availability of relatively low-cost fast food establishments.[37]

With the exception of a brief period following the end of World War II, the portion of the national food budget spent on food consumption away from the home has steadily increased from 9% in 1900 to an estimated 49% in 2008. This phenomenon has important implications for consumer responsiveness to price and income changes, as well as for household nutrition.

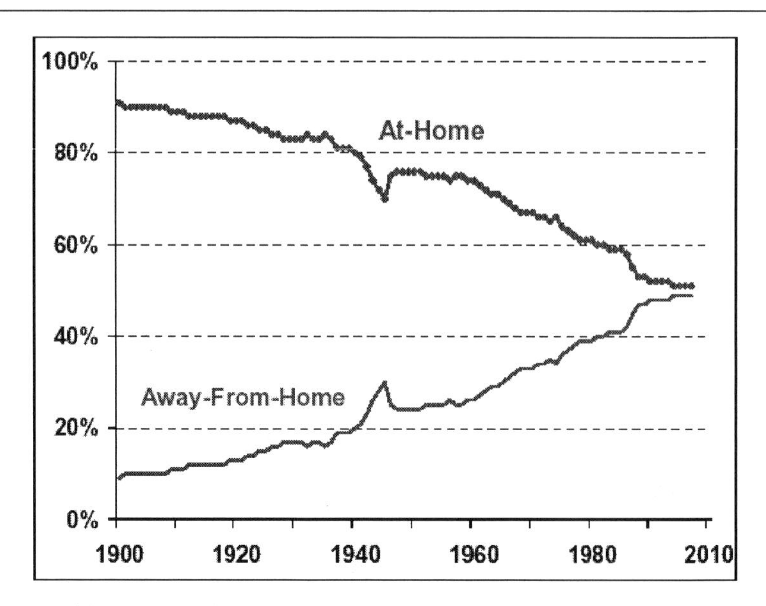


Source: Table 7, "Food CPI, Prices and Expenditures Briefing Room," Food Expenditure Tables, ERS, USDA, available at http://www.ers.usda.gov/Briefing/CPIFoodAndExpenditures/Data/.

Figure 5. Average U.S. Food Expenditure Shares: At-Home vs. Away-from-Home.

The prices of food-at-home purchases are significantly more volatile than are prices of foodaway-from-home purchases (**Table 1 and Figure 6**). ERS research suggests that away-from-home expenditures are typically higher for single-person households and households containing multiple adults without living-at-home children.[38] By implication, households with living-at-home children typically rely more on at-home food consumption (as a share of their budget) and are thus more vulnerable to the normally higher price variability associated with retail food prices.

Although increased food-away-from-home expenditure is associated with higher income (both in absolute terms and as a share of the household food budget), it is not always a luxury item. A partial key to understanding how increasing food-away-from-home consumption may impact consumer behavior is the extent to which such consumption is a choice (for example, made in the evenings or on weekends during leisure hours) or more of an obligation (made during work hours), as well as the extent to which a consumer has alternative dining choices when eating out (for example, subsidized cafeteria meals are often available at schools or in large institutional work settings).

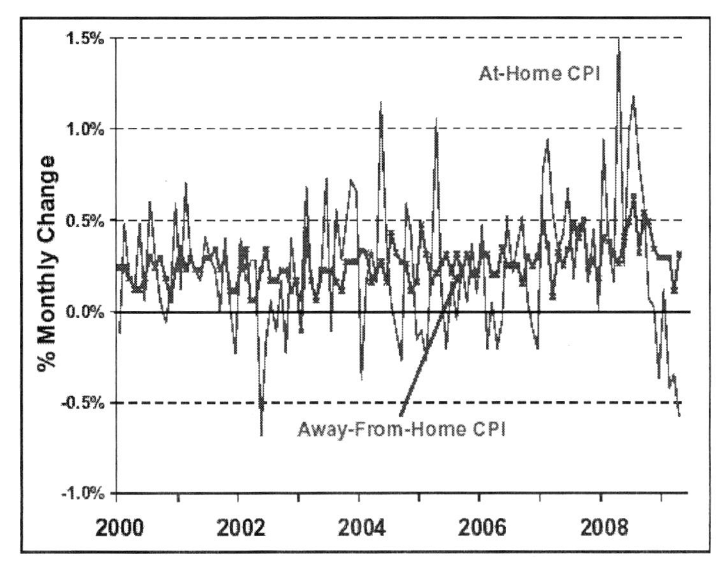


Source: BLS, U.S. Dept. of Labor.

Notes: Month-to-month inflation measured as the percent change in the monthly seasonally adjusted CPI for each index.

Figure 6. Monthly Food Price Inflation Since 2000: At-Home vs. Away-from-Home.

## International Comparisons

The Economic Research Service (ERS) includes in its food expenditure data series a comparison of food budget shares (based on at-home food expenditures) for over 70 countries. **Table 3** includes samples of countries from the ERS database ranked in terms of their at-home food expenditure budget shares, from smallest to largest. These data suggest that, on average, the United States has achieved a higher level of social welfare (based on this particular indicator) than any of the other countries in the database.

The food budget share is only one indicator of national welfare, and it ignores any unfavorable distribution of the food expenditure share (should any exist). Referring back to **Table 2** for the at-home food budget share for U.S. income and total expenditure quintiles based on CES data, it would appear that even the lowest 20% of U.S. households, on average, spend less than 10% of their budgets on at-home food consumption and thus appear relatively well-off in food terms based on this particular international standard. Readers should note that this cursory assessment is aggregate in nature and does not exclude the possibility that there are food-deficient individuals within the lowest 20% quintile of the U.S. population. According to ERS, in 2007, an estimated 11.1% of U.S. households were food-insecure at least some time during the course of the year.[39]

**Table 3. International Comparison of Food-at-Home Budget Shares, 2007**

| Country | Total Expenditures per capita | At-Home Food Expenditures per capita | At-Home Food Share |
|---|---|---|---|
| United States | $33,947 | $1,935 | 5.7% |
| United Kingdom | $27,272 | $2,351 | 8.6% |
| Canada | $23,993 | $2,203 | 9.2% |
| Germany | $21,832 | $2,497 | 11.4% |
| France | $23,184 | $3,176 | 13.7% |
| Italy | $21,315 | $3,091 | 14.5% |
| Japan | $18,737 | $2,742 | 14.6% |
| South Korea | $10,287 | $1,589 | 15.4% |
| Poland | $6,675 | $1,375 | 20.6% |
| Mexico | $5,579 | $1,348 | 24.2% |
| Brazil | $4,183 | $1,028 | 24.6% |
| Russia | $4,363 | $1,251 | 28.7% |
| India | $536 | $174 | 32.4% |
| China | $882 | $308 | 34.9% |
| Philippines | $1,136 | $424 | 37.3% |
| Egypt | $1,279 | $496 | 38.8% |
| Nigeria | $677 | $273 | 40.3% |
| Algeria | $1,119 | $491 | 43.9% |
| Indonesia | $1,138 | $520 | 45.7% |
| Pakistan | $634 | $290 | 45.7% |

Source: Table 97, "Food CPI, Prices and Expenditures Briefing Room," Food Expenditure Tables, ERS, USDA, available at http://www.ers.usda.gov/Briefing/CPIFoodAndExpenditures/Data/.

# RECENT FOOD PRICE INFLATION

This section provides a discussion of observed food price inflation in recent years based on CPI data. It is important to remember that the various CPI categories discussed here are indicative of price changes at the retail level in U.S. urban settings. As such, they are indicative of the prices faced by most consumers living in the United States (approximately 87% of U.S. consumers are covered by the CPI data collection process).

## Annual All-Food versus All-Items Price Inflation

As a general rule, the all-item and all-food CPIs tend to move together. Following a relatively tumultuous period of price inflation in the late 1980s, both price indexes entered an extended period of relative stability. From 1991 through 2006, the all-food CPI measured average annual inflation of 2.5%, compared with 2.7% annual average all-items price inflation.

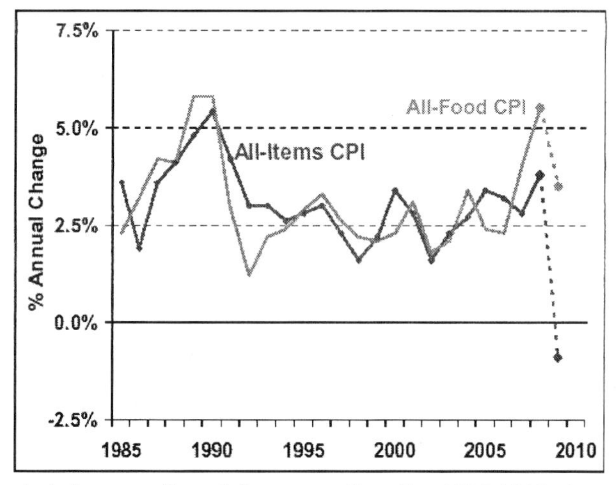


Source: Historical data, unadjusted for seasonality, For 1985-2008, data are from the Dept. of Labor, BLS. Data are forecast for 2009: all-food CPI is from USDA, ERS, as of May 20, 2009; all-items CPI is from Global Insights, U.S. Economic Outlook, June 2009.

Notes: The percent change is calculated from the annual average CPI for successive years.

Figure 7. Annual Price Inflation: All-Items vs. All-Food, 1 985-2009F.

However, several economic factors emerged in late 2005 that began to gradually push market prices higher for both raw agricultural commodities and energy costs.[40] These factors included rising consumer incomes, not just in the United States but globally, which sparked demand for meat and dairy products, food and feed grains, and raw materials ranging from minerals and metals to coal and petroleum. In 2007, U.S. food price inflation reached 4% (**Figure 8**), the highest since 1990.

In early 2008, monthly food price inflation appeared to be accelerating (**Figure 9**). In July 2008, the month-to-month food price change was 0.96% (equivalent to an annual rate of 12.1% if sustained for the entire year). Monthly retail food price inflation responds with a lag of several months to price changes in raw commodity markets. For the entire year, 2008 food prices rose by 5.5%, well above the all-items CPI of 3.8% (**Figure 7**). However, by late 2008 retail price trends had reversed and began following prices for raw agricultural commodities, which had already started to decline by late spring of 2008. By November 2008 monthly retail food price inflation had fallen to near 0%, then actually declined in February and March 2009.

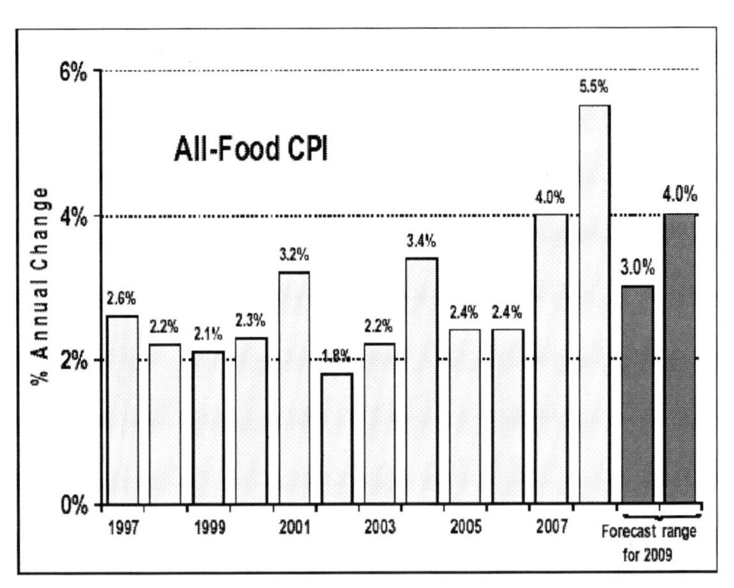


Source: Historical data (1985-2008) are from the Dept. of Labor, BLS. Forecast for the 2009 all-food CPI is from USDA, ERS, May 20, 2009.

Figure 8. Annual Food Price Inflation Since 1997.

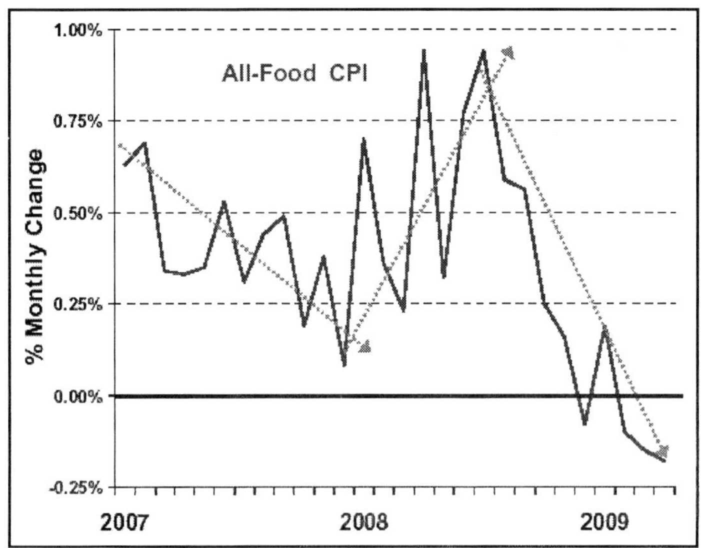


Source: Data, adjusted for seasonality, are from the Department of Labor, BLS.

Notes: The percent change is calculated from the CPI for successive months. Multiply any given month's value by 12 to approximate the annual inflation rate experienced during that particular month, without compounding.

Figure 9. Monthly Retail Food Price Inflation Trended Down in 2007, Spiked Sharply Higher in Early 2008, Then Plummeted into 2009

### *The 2009 Forecast for Annual Food Price Inflation*

In 2009, both price indexes, the all-food and the all-items, are forecast sharply lower (**Figure 7**); however, the all-items CPI is expected to be subject to much stronger deflationary pressures than the all-food CPI. As a result, the disparity between the two indexes is forecast to widen as the all-items CPI falls at an annual rate of -0.9%,[41] while U.S. food price inflation in 2009 is projected by ERS to be in the 3% to 4% range (**Figure 8**).[42] Sharply lower commodity and energy costs are expected to combine with weak domestic and global economies to reduce inflationary pressures from 2008 levels for both of these price indexes. As a result, pressure on retail food prices is expected to subside, resulting in low to moderate food price inflation in 2009.

### *The Recent Monthly All-Food Price Inflation Pattern*

When the all-food CPI is adjusted for seasonal variations and expressed on a monthly basis, three strong patterns can be seen to have emerged since

January 2007 (**Figure 9**). First, a mildly volatile, downward pattern of monthly price change persisted throughout 2007. This was followed by a highly volatile, upward pattern of price inflation during the first nine months of 2008, at which point monthly price changes declined sharply into December, when they actually fell below the preceding month's level (i.e., the monthly all-food CPI deflated or become negative) for the first time since November 2006. Monthly food price changes were again negative in February, March, and April of 2009.

According to ERS, additional month-to-month retail food price declines are possible in early 2009.[43] This is because food processors and retailers are traditionally slow to pass on price decreases that they experience at the wholesale level for several reasons, including substantial inherent operating risk associated with volatile markets.[44]

The same monthly all-food price inflation measures (also adjusted for seasonality) are presented in **Figure 10**, but for a longer time period and accompanied by their 11-month moving average (MA).[45] The MA series reveals a strong upward inflationary trend that began at the end of 2005 and persisted through June 2008. Since June 2008, the MA has moved strongly downward. Retail food prices are clearly responding to the deflationary pressures associated with the collapse of U.S. and international commodity prices that occurred in mid-2008, as well as to the crisis that emerged in late 2008 in U.S. and global financial markets.

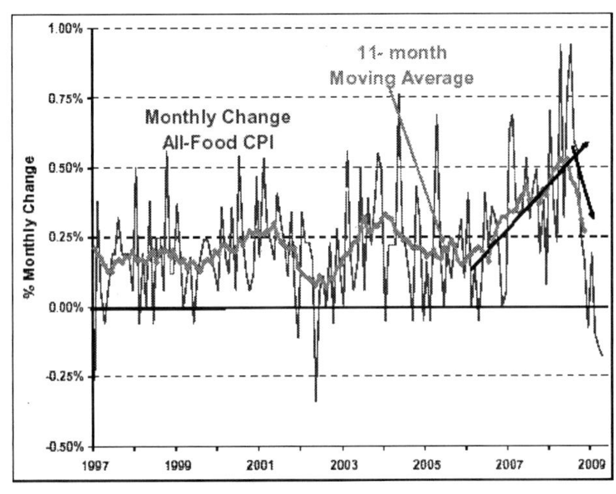


Source: Data, adjusted for seasonality, are from the Department of Labor, BLS.

Figure 10. Food Price Inflation Since 1997: Monthly Change vs. 11-Mo. Moving Ave.

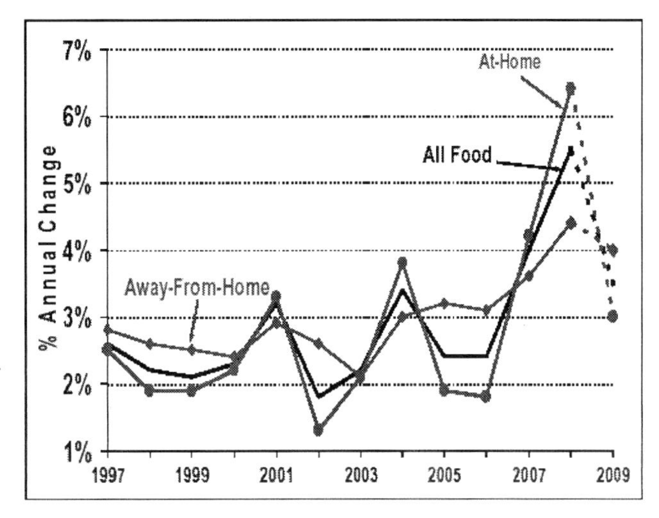


Source: See source info from Table 4.

Figure 11 . Annual Food Price Inflation for All, At-Home, and Away-from-Home CPI (historical data since 1997, with forecast for 2009).

## At-Home versus Away-from-Home Food Price Inflation

As shown earlier (**Figure 6**), at-home food prices are substantially more volatile than away-fromhome food prices (see also **Table 1**, where the at-home food price SD of 1.6% compares with a 0.9% SD for away-from-home food prices since 1983). This volatility is apparent, even when using a shorter time period (**Table 4 and Figure 11**). It is not surprising, then, that at-home food prices are forecast to make a steeper decline in 2009 than either all-food or food-away-from-home, falling from a 6.4% rate of inflation in 2008 to a range of 2.5% to 3.5%.

When displayed in terms of monthly price changes, the pattern exhibited by at-home food price inflation (**Figure 12**) appears very similar to the pattern for all-food price inflation (**Figure 9**), although the at-home food price movements are more extreme. In contrast, monthly away-fromhome price inflation is much more stable. Note that both at-home and away-from-home monthly price inflation show a distinct downturn beginning in July 2008.

**Table 4. Annual Food Price Inflation Since 2005**

| | | Annual % Change | | | | |
|---|---|---|---|---|---|---|
| **Category** | **Weights** | **2005** | **2006** | **2007** | **2008** | **2009F** |
| **All-Items** | **na** | **3.4** | **3.2** | **2.8** | **3.8** | **-0.9** |
| All-Food | 100% | 2.4 | 2.4 | 4.0 | 5.5 | 3.0 to 4.0 |
| Food-at-Home | 55.8% | 1.9 | 1.7 | 4.2 | 6.4 | 2.5 to 3.5 |
| Food-Away-from-Home | 44.3% | 3.1 | 3.1 | 3.6 | 4.4 | 3.5 to 4.5 |

Source: Historical data (unadjusted for seasonality) for 2005 to 2008 are from BLS, Dept of Labor; 2009 forecasts are from ERS, USDA, as of May 20, 2009, at http://www.ers.usda.gov/Briefing/CPIFoodAndExpenditures/Data/cpiforecasts.htm. The all-items CPI forecast for 2009 is from Global Insights, U.S. Economic Outlook, June 2009.

Notes: BLS data are as of February 2009 using 2005-2006 weights for U.S. City Average (CPI-U). Annual percent changes are calculated from annual average indexes.

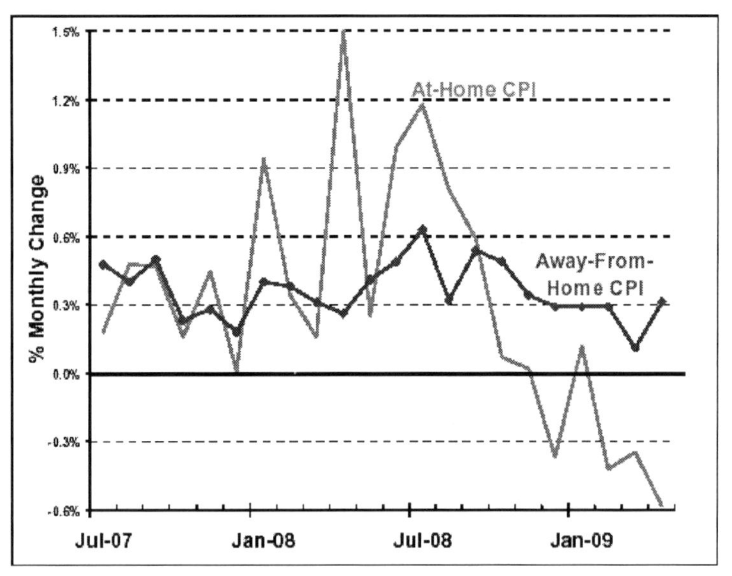


Source: Historical data (adjusted for seasonality) are from BLS, Dept of Labor.

Notes: The percent change is calculated from the CPI for successive months. Multiply any given month's value by 12 to approximate the annual inflation rate experienced during that particular month, without compounding.

Figure 12. Monthly Retail Food Price Inflation Since July 2007 (at-home vs. away-from-home).

## Price Inflation by Major Food Categories

The relatively high food price inflation of 2007 and 2008 was not felt evenly across all food groups, but varied widely in terms of both the timing and the relative magnitude of inflation. In 2008, the inflation rate for at-home food was 6.4% (**Table 5**); however, only the "fruits and vegetables" category experienced a similar level of price inflation (6.2%). Several product categories experienced substantially higher inflation, including egg prices which were up 14% in 2008 after having soared by 29% in 2007; fats and oils were up 13.8%, cereals and bakery products up 10.2%, snacks up 8.1%, and dairy products up 8%. In contrast, the broad price index of meats, poultry, and fish was up only 4.2%, and non-alcoholic beverages (including carbonated and non-carbonated drinks and juices) were up 4.3%.

**Table 5. The Food-at-Home CPI by Category Since 2005**

| | **Weights[a]** | | **Annual Percent Change** | | | | |
|---|---|---|---|---|---|---|---|
| **Category** | **%** | **%** | **2005** | **2006** | **2007** | **2008** | **2009F** |
| **Food at Home** | **100%** | | **1.9** | **1.7** | **4.2** | **6.4** | **2.5 to 3.5** |
| 1-Cereal & Bakery Products | 14.1% | | 1.5 | 1.8 | 4.4 | 10.2 | 2.5 to 3.5 |
| Cereals and products[b] | | 4.5% | 0.3 | 0.3 | 3.9 | 10.1 | na |
| Bakery products[c] | | 9.4% | 2.0 | 2.6 | 4.5 | 10.3 | na |
| 2-Meats; Poultry; & Fish | 21.9% | | 2.4 | 0.8 | 3.8 | 4.2 | 2.0 to 3.0 |
| Beef & veal | | 6.8% | 2.6 | 0.8 | 4.5 | 4.5 | 1.5 to 2.5 |
| Pork | | 4.2% | 2.0 | -0.3 | 2.0 | 2.3 | 1.5 to 2.5 |
| Poultry | | 4.1% | 2.0 | -1.8 | 5.2 | 5.0 | 2.0 to 3.0 |
| Fish & seafood | | 3.7% | 3.0 | 4.7 | 4.6 | 6.0 | 4.0 to 5.0 |
| 3-Eggs | 1.3% | | -13.7 | 4.9 | 29.2 | 14.0 | -5.0 to - 4.0 |
| 4-Dairy & Products | 11.2% | | 1.2 | -0.6 | 7.4 | 8.0 | -4.0 to -3.0 |
| Milk | | 3.8% | 1.6 | -1.2 | 11.7 | 6.0 | na |
| Cheese | | 3.6% | 1.4 | -1.4 | 5.9 | 12.1 | na |
| Ice Cream | | 1.8% | -0.4 | 0.9 | 2.3 | 5.1 | na |
| Other | | 2.0% | 1.6 | 0.6 | 6.1 | 7.7 | na |
| 5-Fruits & Vegetables | 14.6% | | 3.7 | 4.8 | 3.8 | 6.2 | 3.0 to 4.0 |

Table 5. (Continued)

| | Weights[a] | | Annual Percent Change | | | | |
|---|---|---|---|---|---|---|---|
| **Category** | **%** | **%** | **2005** | **2006** | **2007** | **2008** | **2009F** |
| Fresh fruits | | 5.6% | 3.7 | 6.0 | 4.5 | 4.8 | 3.0 to 4.0 |
| Fresh vegetables | | 5.6% | 4.0 | 4.6 | 3.2 | 5.6 | 3.0 to 4.0 |
| Processed fruits & veg. | | 3.5% | 3.3 | 2.9 | 3.6 | 9.5 | 3.0 to 4.0 |
| 6-Non-alcoholic Beverages | 12.0% | | 2.9 | 2.0 | 4.1 | 4.3 | 3.0 to 4.0 |
| Juices & non-alc. drinks | | 8.0% | 1.9 | 2.3 | 4.2 | 4.4 | na |
| Coffee, tea, & other | | 4.1% | 5.0 | 1.6 | 4.0 | 4.2 | na |
| 7-Sugar & Sweets | 3.7% | | 1.2 | 3.8 | 3.1 | 5.5 | 3.0 to 4.0 |
| 8-Fats & Oils | 3.0% | | 0.0 | 0.2 | 2.9 | 13.8 | 3.0 to 4.0 |
| 8-Other Foods[d] | 18.2% | | 1.5 | 1.4 | 1.8 | 5.2 | 3.0 to 4.0 |
| Froz./freeze-dried foods | | 3.8% | 0.5 | 0.4 | 1.9 | 4.3 | na |
| Snacks | | 3.8% | 2.8 | 1.5 | 2.0 | 8.1 | na |

Source: Historical data for 2005 to 2008 are from BLS, Department of Labor, as of May 2009, for the U.S. City Average (CPI-U). The 2009 forecasts are from ERS, USDA, as of May 20, 2009. For the most recent forecast, visit http://www.ers.usda.gov/Briefing/CPIFoodAndExpenditures/Data/cpiforecasts.htm

a. Weights are "as a percent of total at-home food expenditures."

b. Flour and prepared flour mixes, breakfast cereals, rice, pasta, and cornmeal.

c. Bread, fresh biscuits, rolls, muffins, cakes, cupcakes, cookies, and other bakery products.

d. Includes soups, spices, seasonings, condiments, sauces, baby food, and other miscellaneous foods.

The demand-side influences of income growth (and decline) and the global financial crisis that emerged in late 2008 have already been discussed briefly. On the supply side, food price inflation is the result of dynamic forces that occur both at the farm where the raw agricultural ingredients for retail food items are produced, and along the marketing chain as the farm output is transformed and moved to the retail customer. An array of costs are layered on top of the price of the raw agricultural commodity, including handling, transportation, storage, and processing, as well as the insurance, financing, and advertising costs necessary to move the product to the retail customer. The relative importance of these marketing costs varies widely for different retail food products depending on the degree of processing and transformation (i.e., cleaning, packaging, shipping, advertising, etc.). As a result, economic forces such as higher energy costs or increased labor rates do not impact all food categories equally.

In 2009, at-home food prices are forecast to rise a modest 3% (within a range of 2.5% to 3.5%). However, eggs and dairy products are forecast to fall sharply from their 2008 levels—egg prices are forecast to fall by 4.5% (in a range of -5% to -4%), and dairy products are forecast down by 3.5% (in a range of -4% to -3%).

Annual averages can cloud over substantial inter-year price movements. As a result, it is often worthwhile to glance over the monthly price indexes for the past two years to get a better sense of the general pattern of retail food price movements across the various food groups. Monthly price indexes (**Figure 13**) for the four principal food groups—cereals and bakery products; meats (including beef, pork, poultry, and seafood); dairy products (including milk, cheese, ice cream, and other); and fruits and vegetables (including fresh as well as processed)—for the period from January 2007 through April 2009 reveal very different patterns of price movement.[46]

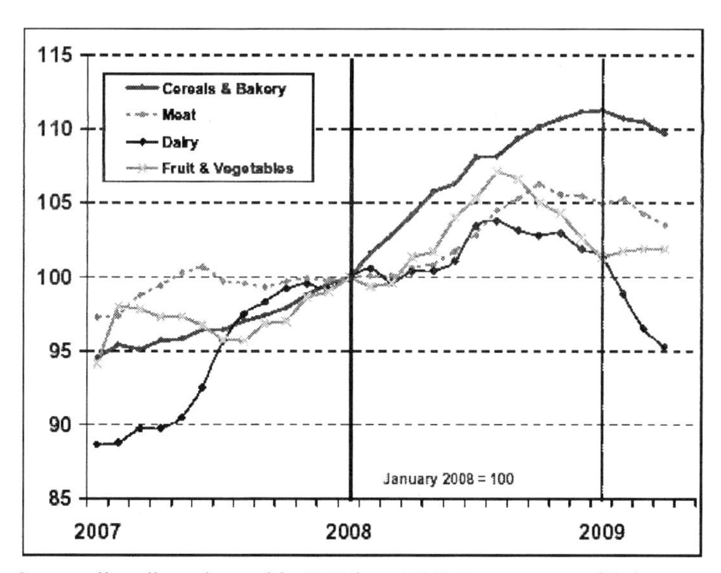


Source: Seasonally adjusted monthly CPI data, BLS, Department of Labor.

Figure 13. Monthly Retail Price Indexes: Various Major Food Groups.

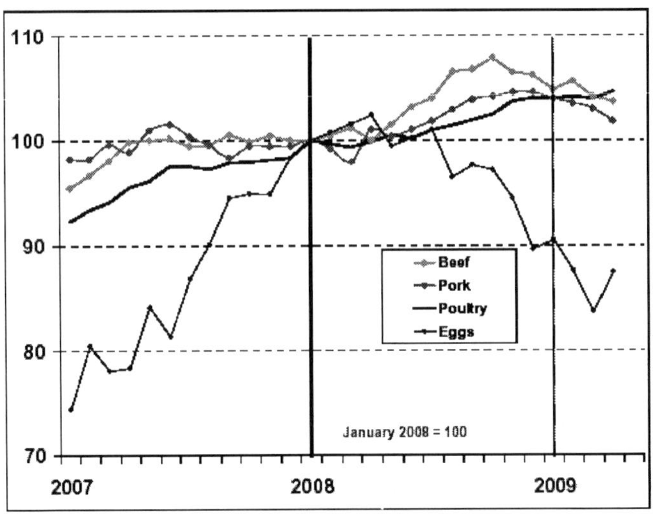


Source: Seasonally adjusted monthly CPI data, BLS, Department of Labor.

Figure 14. Monthly Retail Price Indexes: Beef, Pork, Poultry, and Eggs.

The meat price index was the most stable over this period, while the cereals and bakery product price index showed the strongest increase, rising nearly 18% between January 2007 and January 2009. The dairy price index showed a strong rise through 2007 and into 2008, then declined slightly through the second half of 2008 before falling sharply in early 2009 (down 6.5% since December 2008). The fruit and vegetable price index was the most volatile, as a general upward pattern over the two-year period was punctuated by significant deflationary movements during both 2007 and 2008.

Perhaps the most dramatic and volatile of the individual foods was eggs (**Figure 14**), which rose 35% from January 2007 to January 2008, then fell over 16% by February 2009. A year-over-year production decline from 2006 to 2007 coupled with strong exports tightened U.S. egg supplies and pushed prices sharply higher. Stronger egg production by mid-2008 coupled with the global economic crisis dampened prices in the later half of 2008.

The components of the dairy group (**Figure 15**) followed distinctly different patterns, particularly the price index for fresh milk, which showed a sharp escalation in early 2007 (up 20%), followed by a sharp drop-off in 2008 including a 19.5% fall from July 2008 to April 2009. The milk price pattern for the 2007-2008 period was very similar to the egg price pattern for that same period, and for the same principal reasons—initially tight supplies and expensive feed costs, followed by increased supplies and a sharp drop in prices and demand. U.S. milk production expanded through 2007 and into 2008, while the global economic crisis weakened demand, especially from international markets. In contrast, highly processed ice cream showed a fairly steady upward rise from mid-2007 before slowing in early 2009.

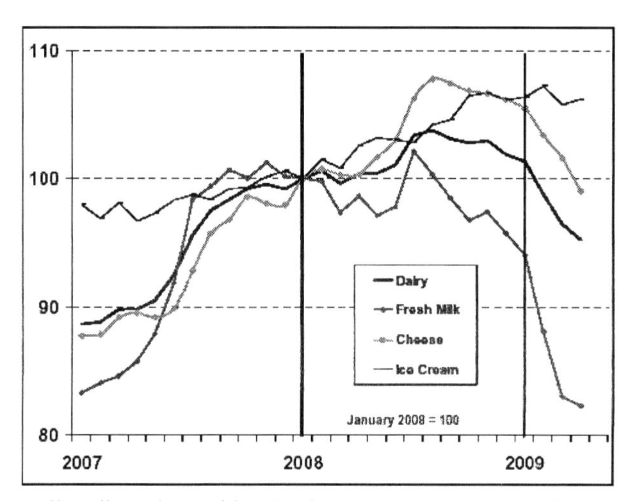


Source: Seasonally adjusted monthly CPI data, BLS, Department of Labor.

Figure 15. Monthly Retail Price Indexes: Dairy, Fresh Milk, Cheese, and Ice Cream.

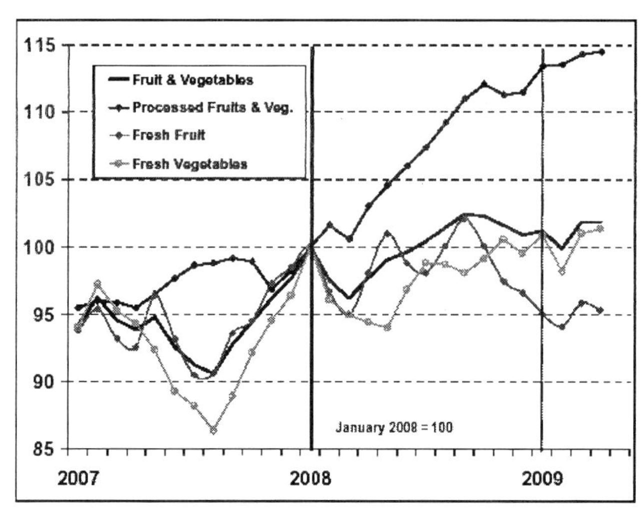


Source: Seasonally adjusted monthly CPI data, BLS, Department of Labor.

Figure 16. Monthly Retail Price Indexes: Fruits and Vegetables.

Similarly, the price index for processed fruits and vegetables (**Figure 16**) rose steadily through 2008, while the price indexes for fresh fruit and fresh vegetables exhibited volatile, slightly upward patterns.

The price index for highly processed snacks (**Figure 17**) rose slowly in 2007, then accelerated upward during 2008. The sugar and sweets price index had a similar pattern, although with a somewhat slower rise during 2008. The fats and oils price index rose rapidly during 2007 and during the first nine months of 2008, then leveled off as the global market for oils became over-supplied, in part due to the fall-off in demand (related to the global financial crisis) in lesser-developed countries, where fats and oils are still treated as luxury goods.

Similar to other highly processed food products, the prepared-food group (which includes frozen and freeze-dried prepared foods) and the carbonated beverages index both rose steadily through 2008 (**Figure 18**). However, both the prepared foods and carbonated beverages price indexes showed signs of leveling off in early 2009. In contrast, coffee prices rose sharply during the first half of 2008 before falling sharply in response to a decline in demand following the global financial crisis.

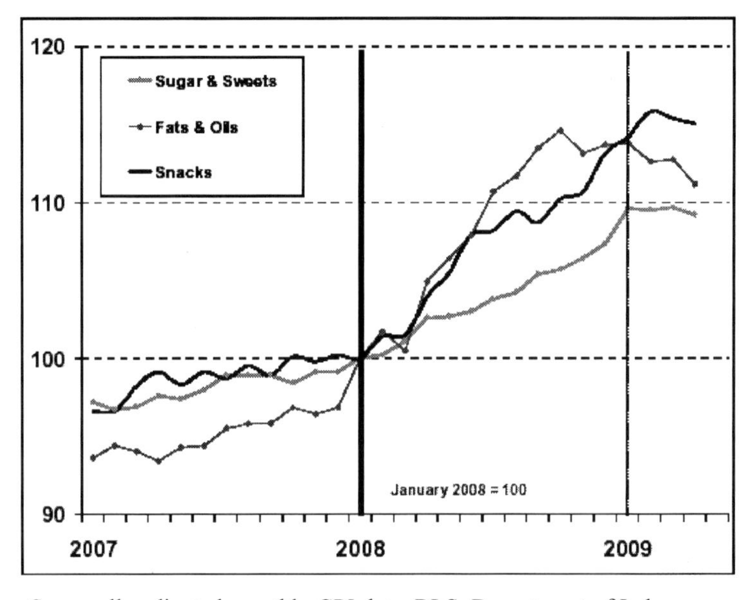


Source: Seasonally adjusted monthly CPI data, BLS, Department of Labor.

Figure 17. Monthly Retail Price Indexes: Sugar, Fat & Oils, and Snacks.

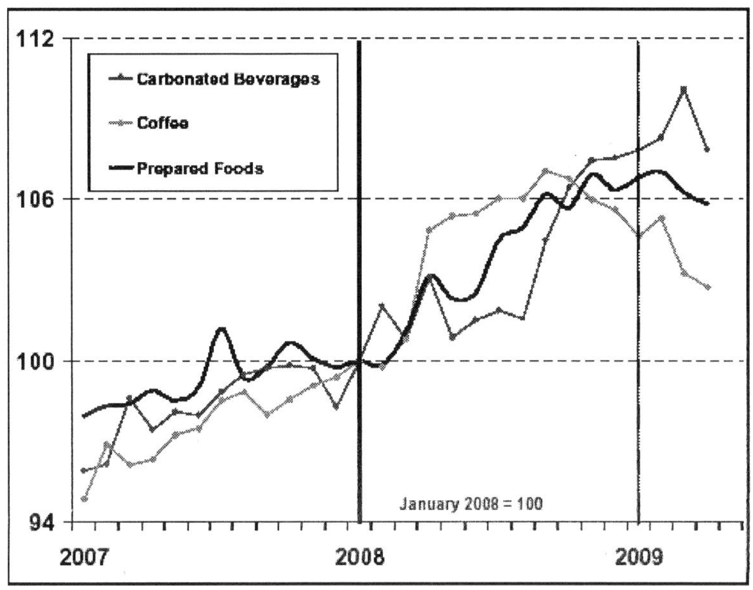


Source: Seasonally adjusted monthly CPI data, BLS, Department of Labor.

Figure 18. Monthly Retail Price Indexes: Coffee, Carbonated Beverages, and Prepared Foods.

In sum, evidence from recent years suggests that highly processed foods more consistently adhere to steady, stable upward price trends. In contrast, prices for less-processed retail food products—such as eggs, milk, and fresh fruits and vegetables—respond far more quickly to changes in both farm commodity prices and economic conditions and have followed farm prices downward in the early months of 2009.

## EFFECT OF HIGH PRICES

The surge in agricultural commodity prices as well as the rise in costs of raw materials, energy, and transportation that persisted from mid-2005 through early 2008 translated into higher retail prices for food and other household products. For a given level of income, higher prices mean lower effective purchasing power, since the same household budget will now acquire a smaller volume of products.

Many wages and salaries, as well as federal programs (including several domestic food assistance programs), are linked to price inflation through escalation clauses in order to retain their purchasing power. For households where income does not keep up with price inflation, declines in purchasing power are both real and immediate. However, even for households with escalation clauses that adjust incomes or benefits for price inflation, there is a time lag between the time the price inflation is measured and the time when the wage or program benefit is adjusted upward to compensate. As a result, for households with incomes or federal benefits linked to price inflation escalators, higher prices can cause a short-term decline in real purchasing power. This is most meaningful when prices are accelerating. When prices are falling, as during a deflationary period, consumers with fixed incomes realize gains in real income (provided that they are not subject to wage cuts or layoffs).

Although commodity prices peaked in early 2008 and have been declining since, most retail prices have been slow to reflect wholesale commodity price declines, and it has only been since early 2009 that retail prices have significantly retreated for most foods. The negative aspects of high retail prices have been magnified by the global financial crisis that emerged in 2008. The economic downturn has manifested itself in a decline in household wealth due to sharply lower real estate values, tighter business and consumer credit, and rising unemployment numbers.

## Federal Spending for Domestic Food Assistance Programs

The federal government operates several domestic food assistance programs targeted to low-income households, as well as schoolchildren and nutritionally vulnerable groups such as pregnant and/or lactating mothers.[47]

Food price inflation leads to more spending on domestic assistance efforts. Increasing prices encourage those who are eligible, but not participating, to enroll. They also translate directly (albeit with a time lag) into higher benefit payments and per-meal subsidies for "entitlement" programs in which benefits are indexed to food-price inflation. These entitlement programs include the Supplemental Nutrition Assistance Program (the SNAP, formerly the Food Stamp Program) and programs supporting meals served to children in schools and other venues. Increasing prices also place pressure on appropriators to provide more funding to support caseloads for "discretionary" programs like the Special Supplemental Nutrition Program for Women, Infants, and Children (the WIC program).

The 2008-2009 global economic crisis—with its higher unemployment, income loss, and lower effective household purchasing power—following on the heels of higher retail prices, has brought on higher participation rates and greater costs for domestic food aid programs like the SNAP, child nutrition meal-service programs (e.g., the School Lunch program), the WIC program, The Emergency Food Assistance Program (TEFAP), and Older Americans Act nutrition programs. As of January 2009 (the latest available information to date), participation in the SNAP was at an all- time record high of 32.2 million persons (or about one in every 10 Americans). SNAP monthly benefit costs have grown from $2.8 billion in January 2008 to $3.6 billion in January 2009, with average per-person monthly benefit spending rising from $100 to $113. Other domestic food assistance programs also have seen increased participation (and costs). The number of lower- income children receiving free or reduced-price school lunches has risen from 18.2 million schoolchildren in January 2008 to 19.3 million in January 2009. WIC participation has grown from 8.6 million women, infants, and children in January 2008 to some 9 million in January 2009.

Responding to calls for increased federal assistance, the 2009 American Recovery and Reinvestment Act (ARRA; P.L. 111-5) provided additional support for domestic food assistance programs: an estimated $11.5 billion for FY2009-FY2010 and $20.8 billion through FY2019.[48] The SNAP is the primary recipient of this new money, most of which will be used to pay for added benefits, loosened eligibility standards, and administrative costs.

## Supplemental Nutrition Assistance Program (SNAP, formerly Food Stamps)

The SNAP is the largest of the federally supported domestic food assistance programs. SNAP benefits normally are indexed annually (each October) for changes in the cost of USDA's least costly food plan, the "Thrifty Food Plan" (TFP). For a number of years and well into 2006, annual increases in the cost of the TFP typically ranged between 1.5% and 2.5%. However, starting in late 2006, food prices reflected in the cost of items in the TFP began to increase at a much faster rate. For example, basic benefits were increased by 4.6% in FY2007 and by 8.5% in October 2008. While these were substantial increases, they lagged by three months in reflecting rising food costs—they were (by law) based on prices from the immediately previous June. Thus there is a three-month gap between the calculation of the price inflation index in June and its use to adjust SNAP benefits in October.

In recognition of the lag in the inflation index for SNAP benefits, increased food needs, and reduced income, the ARRA included a major across-the-board boost in SNAP benefits, effective in April 2009. The ARRA provisions mandate that the TFP dollar amounts used for basic SNAP benefits be 13.6% above the June 2008 TFP cost level; this effectively boosts each recipient household's monthly benefit by an amount equal to 13.6% of the maximum (TFP) benefit for its household size. For a one-person household, the added benefit is $24 a month; for two persons, $44 a month; for three persons (the typical household), $63 a month; for four persons, $80 a month; and for larger households, higher amounts. This change adds to the already effective 8.5% increase in benefits under pre-existing law. For example, inflation-indexed monthly benefits for four-person households went up by $46 in October 2008 (the 8.5% increase mentioned above); the ARRA adds another $80 a month. However, the structure of the ARRA increase is such that the new, higher benefit levels will continue until normal annual indexing rules provide benefits that surpass the value of the new add-on. As a result, it is unlikely that there will be another SNAP benefit increase related to food costs until October 2010 or later, unless food prices increase dramatically.[49]

The impact of benefit increases on SNAP costs also depends on participation. The number of Americans receiving SNAP assistance has climbed steadily over the past eight years from a low of about 17.2 million in 2000 to an all-time record high of 33.2 million in March 2009. The previous food stamp participation peak was in 1994, when about 27.5 million Americans received assistance.

For FY2008, the regular benefit increase noted above (combined with estimated growth in enrollment) yielded a likely $2 billion cost attributable to adjustments for food price increases (out of total spending of $36.7 billion), about double the $1 billion that would have occurred based on pre-2007 price increases. Costs are expected to increase even more in FY2009.

### *Child Nutrition*

Federally supported child nutrition programs and initiatives reach more than 40 million children. In FY2008, federal spending on these programs totaled over $15 billion, the second-largest federal commitment to domestic food assistance. The basic goals of federal child nutrition programs are to improve children's nutrition, increase lower-income children's access to nutritious meals and snacks, and help support the agricultural economy.

Federal payments for meals and snacks served to children now range as high as $2.80 per meal, including the value of USDA commodity donations. Cash per-meal payments are indexed every July to food-price changes reflected in the food-away-from-home component of the CPI over the 12-month period ending each May. Commodity support (now some 21 cents per meal) also is indexed annually based on the Bureau of Labor Statistics' Producer Price Index for five major food components (cereal and bakery products, meats, poultry and fish, dairy products, processed fruits and vegetables, and fats and oils).

Inflation-indexed subsidy rates (those paid for the majority of school meals that are served free or at a reduced price to children from lower-income families) have increased by over 35 cents per meal between the 2005-2006 school year and the current 2008-2009 school year. The annual increase in subsidies has gone from 2.9% for the 2005-2006 school year to 3.3% for the 2007-2008 school year and well over 4% for the 2008-2009 school year; in FY2008, this increased federal support by about $300 million above spending if earlier food price increases had prevailed. This trend is expected to continue into FY2009.

While inflation indexing of child nutrition subsidies lags behind actual increased costs to participating meal providers like schools, no change has been made to the annual July indexing cycle.

### *The WIC Program*

Unlike the SNAP and child nutrition programs, which receive mandatory funding, the WIC program is funded from discretionary sources. Spending depends on annual appropriations, based largely on estimates of participation and the cost of the food packages that are purchased with WIC vouchers. The value of benefits is not indexed, per se. Rather, WIC vouchers are redeemable at whatever the participating retailer charges for the items covered by the vouchers, which differ according to the type of recipient (e.g., pregnant mother, infant, child). As a result, the cost of WIC vouchers reflect food price changes without the time lag built into other inflation-indexed nutrition programs. Just as important, WIC vouchers are highly specific as to the food items they cover and have a relatively heavy emphasis on certain types of food—for example, dairy items and infant formula are major components.

In recent years, the cost of WIC food vouchers has varied a great deal, largely because of changes in dairy-related food prices. The average per-participant monthly cost of vouchers has ranged from $34.80 in FY2002 to $39.15 in FY2007. However, the annual percentage increase has been very small for some years (1% or less for FY2003, FY2005, and FY2006) and more substantial for other years (6.6% for FY2004 and 5.6% for FY2007). Most recently, monthly per-participant WIC food costs averaged just under $45 for the first three months of FY2009, compared to about $42 for the same period last year. Given this significant volatility, it is difficult to produce specific estimates of the effect of food price inflation on WIC program costs.

Although WIC spending is discretionary, Congress has historically shown a willingness to appropriate whatever amounts are necessary to meet costs imposed by increased participation or food costs. Most recently, it provided a $400 million contingency reserve to meet unexpected costs in FY2009 and FY20 10 as part of the ARRA.

### *TEFAP and Older Americans Act Programs*

The Emergency Food Assistance Program (TEFAP) and meal service programs under the Older Americans Act also provide key food assistance support for vulnerable groups. Like the WIC program, they are discretionary, and rising need and higher food prices have placed pressure on appropriators to add to federal funding. TEFAP, which provides federally donated food commodities and supports distribution of privately donated commodities, is budgeted at $450 million in FY2009 ($350 million for commodities and $100 million for distribution costs); as a result of new funding provided by the ARRA, this is $150 million above the amount previously available. Older Americans Act nutrition programs ("meals-on-wheels" and meals served to seniors in congregate meal settings) also have received added funding under the ARRA; $100 million in new FY2009 federal support was added to about $800 million already available.

## Foreign Food Aid

USDA's international activities are funded by discretionary appropriations (e.g., foreign food assistance under the Food for Peace Act (P.L. 480) and by using the borrowing authority of the CCC (e.g., export credit guarantees, market development programs, and export subsidies).[50] Because foreign food aid is a budget value and not a food volume, its effective "purchase power" is diminished by food price hikes without additional appropriations. Unlike some domestic nutrition programs, foreign food aid is not adjusted to account for changing costs.

Food aid usually takes the form of basic food grains such as wheat, sorghum, and corn, and vegetable oil—commodities critical to developing-country diets. Since there is very little value added for these commodities, shifts in prices translate directly into higher prices for food-insecure countries or reduced food aid contributions per dollar spent. Also, higher energy costs have increased shipping costs for both food purchases and food aid.

## Author Contact Information

Randy Schnepf
Specialist in Agricultural
rschnepf@crs.loc.gov, 7-4277

Joe Richardson
Policy Specialist in Social Policy
jirichardson@crs.loc.gov, 7-7325

## End Notes

[1] Examples of food groups include meat, dairy products, bakery goods, fruits, or vegetables.

[2] The PCE price index is a measure of the change in prices paid for goods and services by the personal sector in the U.S. national income and product accounts (NIPA).

[3] Information on both of these bureaus can be obtained by visiting http://www.commerce

[4] For more information on the Census Bureau's income data, visit http://www.census.gov/hhes/www/income

[5] For more information on NIPAs, see *Measuring the Economy: A Primer on GDP and the National Income and Product Accounts*, BEA, U.S. Dept. of Commerce, Sept. 2007, at http://www.bea.gov/national/pdf/nipa_primer.pdf.

[6] ERS undertakes economic research across a broad range of agricultural policy topics not limited to consumer food price and expenditure issues. Information related to food prices and expenditures is accessible at the *Food CPI, Prices, and Expenditures* Briefing Room, at http://www.ers.usda.gov/Briefing/CPIFoodAndExpenditures/.

[7] ERS food price inflation forecasts are available at http://www.ers.usda.gov/Briefing/CPIFoodAndExpenditures/Data/ cpiforecasts.htm.

[8] For a list of the food expenditure tables, visit http://www.ers.usda.gov/Briefing/CPIFoodAndExpenditures/Data/.

[9] "Table 30—Consumer food price indexes and food expenditures," at http://www.ers.usda.gov/Briefing/Baseline/.

[10] For information on entire demand systems, see "Food Demand Analysis," and for information on specific food groups, see "Who Eats What, Where, and How Much," both at the *Diet Quality and Food Consumption* Briefing Room, ERS, USDA, at http://www.ers.usda.gov/Briefing/DietQuality/whoeats.htm.

[11] James Seale, Jr., Anita Regmi, and Jason Bernstein, *International Evidence on Food Consumption Patterns*, Technical Bulletin No. 1904, ERS, USDA, Sept. 2003, and Anita

Regmi, ed., *Changing Structure of Global Food Consumption and Trade*, Agriculture and Trade Report WRS-01-1, ERS, USDA, May 2001.

[12] For more information, see the U.S. Dept. of Labor, BLS, *BLS Handbook of Methods, Chapter 16, Consumer Expenditures and Income*, at http://www.bls.gov/opub/hom/pdf/homch16.pdf.

[13] The BLS releases data from the CES in several formats including an annual report, news releases, and articles in the *Monthly Labor Review* and other journals. For more information on the CES, see the BLS website for "CES Frequently Asked Questions," at http://www.bls.gov/cex/faq.htm.

[14] CPI data, once released, are never revised because of their widespread use for adjusting wages to cost-of-living adjustments. However, the components of the market basket, their respective weights, and the formula for calculating price changes are revised on occasion for future calculations.

[15] For details, see "Measuring the ERS Food Expenditure Series," *Food CPI, Prices, and Expenditures* Briefing Room, ERS, at http://www.ers.usda.gov/Briefing/CPIFoodAndExpenditures/measuringtheersfoodexpenditu resseries.htm.

[16] For more information, see CRS Report RL3 0074, *The Consumer Price Index: A Brief Overview*, by Brian W. Cashell.

[17] The BLS CPI website with supporting documents and news releases is at http://www.bls.gov/cpi.

[18] For more information, see the BLS report, The Consumer Price Index—Why the Published Averages Don't Always Match An Individual's Inflation Experience, at http://www.bls.gov/cpi/cpifact5.htm.

[19] A subset of the U-population, the W-population consists of the U-population for whom 50% or more of household income comes from wages and clerical workers' earnings. The W-population is used to create its own price index (CPI- W). For specific details refer to "Calculation of Price Indexes," *BLS Handbook of Methods, Chapter 17, The Consumer Price Index*, BLS, Dept. of Labor, p. 2, June 2007, at http://www.bls.gov/opub/hom/pdf/homch17.pdf.

[20] "How BLS Measures Changes in Consumer Prices," BLS, Dept of Labor, at http://www.bls.gov/cpi/cpifact2.htm.

[21] For specific details refer to "Calculation of Price Indexes," *BLS Handbook of Methods, Chapter 17, The Consumer Price Index*, BLS, Dept. of Labor, pp. 3-4, June 2007, available at http://www.bls.gov/opub/hom/pdf/homch17.pdf.

[22] All CPI data referenced in this report refer to the CPI-U data series.

[23] For a brief discussion of 1970s energy markets, see CRS Report R401 87, *U.S. Energy: Overview and Selected Facts and Numbers*, by Carl E. Behrens and Carol Glover. For a brief discussion of 1 970s agricultural markets, see May Peters, Suchada Langley, and Paul Westcott, "Agricultural Commodity Price Spikes in the 1970s and 1990s," *Amber Waves*, ERS, USDA, March 2009, at http://www.ers.usda.gov/.

[24] For more information, see CRS Report RS22705, *Inflation: Core vs. Headline*, by Marc Labonte.

[25] This discussion follows from "A Note on Seasonally Adjusted and Unadjusted Data," *Consumer Price Index: February 2009*, monthly news release, BLS, U.S. Department of Labor.

[26] For more information, see CRS Report RL34168, *Automatic Cost of Living Adjustments: Some Economic and Practical Considerations*, by Brian W. Cashell.

[27] This discussion follows from "CPI Bias," *Food CPI, Prices, and Expenditures* Briefing Room, ERS, USDA, as of March 26, 2007, at http://www.ers.usda.gov/Briefing/CPIFoodAndExpenditures/cpibias.htm.

[28] For a discussion of this issue see *The Impact of Big-Box Stores on Retail Food Prices and the Consumer Price Index*, Economic Research Report No. 33, Ephraim Leibtag, ERS, USDA, December 2006.

[29] Empirical studies conducted in the 1980s and 90s suggested that substitution bias resulted in an upward bias of about 0.4 percentage points per year in using changes in the CPI to measure changes in the cost of living. M. Boskin, E. Dulberger, R.J. Gordon, Z. Griliches, and D.W. Jorgenson, "Consumer Prices, the Consumer Price Index, and the Cost of Living," *Journal of Economic Perspectives*, Vol. 12, No. 1, Winter 1998, pp. 3-26.

[30] For more information on the C-CPI-U, see CRS Report RL32293, *The Chained Consumer Price Index: How Is It Different, and Would It Be Appropriate for Cost-of-Living Adjustments?* by Brian W. Cashell.

[31] NIPA data tables including PCE price indexes are available at http://www.bea.gov/national/nipaweb/index.asp.

[32] For a detailed discussion of their differences, see Clinton P. McCully, Brian C. Moyer, and Kenneth J. Stewart, "Comparing the Consumer Price Index and the Personal Consumption Expenditures Price Index," *Survey of Current Business*, November 2007, at http://www.bea.gov/scb/pdf/2007/11%20November/1107_cpipce.pdf.

[33] The CPI is calculated using a "modified" Laspeyres index, while the PCE price index is calculated using the Fisher-Ideal Index. See source information from the preceding footnote 32 for details.

[34] "Personal Income and Outlays: January 2009," News Release BEA 09-06, March 2, 2009. The estimates for 2008 total and per-capita DPI were $10,645.8 billion and $34,958, respectively. However, comparable food expenditure data for 2008 were not yet available as of March 2009.

[35] The DPI and DPI-food-share estimates are for 2007 from Table 7, Food Expenditure Tables, *Food CPI, Prices and Expenditures* Briefing Room, ERS, USDA, at http://www.ers.usda.gov/Briefing/CPIFoodAndExpenditures/Data/.

[36] CES data are calculated "per consumer unit" which is described as "similar to a household" by BLS.

[37] For a discussion of this issue, see "Food Away From Home," *Diet Quality and Food Consumption* Briefing Room, ERS, USDA, at http://www.ers.usda.gov/Briefing/DietQuality/.

[38] Hayden Stewart, Noel Blisard, Sanjib Bhuyan, and Rodolfo M. Nayga, Jr., *The Demand for Food Away From Home: Full-Service or Fast Food?* AER No. 829, ERS, January 2004.

[39] For a discussion of food insecurity in the United States, see *Food Security in the United States* Briefing Room, ERS, USDA, at http://www.ers.usda.gov/Briefing/FoodSecurity/.

[40] For more information on the factors behind the sharp run-up in global commodity prices in the first half of 2008, see CRS Report RL34474, *High Agricultural Commodity Prices: What Are the Issues?* by Randy Schnepf.

[41] The all-items CPI forecast is from *U.S. Executive Summary*, Global Insights, June 2009. The Congressional Budget Office (CBO) forecasts an all-items CPI inflation rate for 2009 of -0.7% in *A Preliminary Analysis of the President's Budget and an Update of CBO 's Budget and Economic Outlook*, CBO, March 2009.

[42] ERS updates its food price forecast monthly. For the most current ERS food price forecast with related data tables and a discussion of the issues, see "Analysis and Forecasts of the CPI for Food," *Food CPI and Expenditures* Briefing Room, ERS, USDA, at http://www.ers.usda.gov/Briefing/CPIFoodAndExpenditures/consumerpriceindex.htm.

[43] ERS analyst Ephraim Leibtag, as quoted in Mike Hughlett, "Food Costs: Prices Starting to Get Reined In," *Chicagotribune.com*, March 27, 2009.

[44] These issues are discussed in more detail in CRS Report R40621, *Farm-to-Food Price Dynamics*, by Randy Schnepf.

[45] Moving averages are used to reveal underlying patterns or trends that can otherwise be hidden by a substantial amount of month-to-month variation in price movements.

[46] Note that these statistics (based on the change in monthly price indexes) differ from the statistics reported in **Table 5**, where the inflation rates are calculated using the difference from annual averages rather than monthly averages.

[47] For details on the individual programs, see "Programs and Services," Food and Nutrition Service, USDA, at http://www.fns.usda.gov/fns/services. Also see CRS Report R40397, *Child Nutrition and WIC Programs: A Brief Overview*, by Joe Richardson. For program funding information, see the "Domestic Food Assistance" section (by Joe Richardson) of CRS Report R40000, *Agriculture and Related Agencies: FY2009 Appropriations*, coordinated by Jim Monke.

[48] For more information, see CRS Report R40 160, *Agriculture, Nutrition, and Rural Provisions in the American Recovery and Reinvestment Act (ARRA) of 2009*, coordinated by Jim Monke.

[49] As of February 2009, the cost of the TFP was just 1% above the base June 2008 TFP.

[50] For more information, see CRS Report RL33553, *Agricultural Export and Food Aid Programs*, by Charles E. Hanrahan.

*Chapter 2*

# FARM-TO-FOOD PRICE DYNAMICS*

*Randy Schnepf*
Agricultural Policy

## SUMMARY

The heightened commodity price volatility of 2008 and the subsequent acceleration in U.S. food price inflation have raised concerns and generated many questions about farm and food price movements from Members of Congress and their constituents. This report responds to those concerns by addressing the linkage between farm and retail food prices. Food price inflation is addressed in CRS Report R40545, *Consumers and Food Price Inflation*.

Price is the primary mechanism that links raw farm commodities through the various levels of the market system to the retail food product. The nature of price transmission between farm and retail levels depends, in general, on the size of the farm-value share of the retail price and the degree of market competition at each stage of the marketing chain.

An array of costs are layered on top of the price of a raw agricultural commodity at each stage of the marketing chain as it moves to the consumer. As a result, the farm-value share of a food product's price declines as it moves

---

* This is an edited, reformatted and augmented version of a CRS Report for Congress publication dated May 2009.

to the retail outlet. Since 1950, the average farm-value share has been declining as a share of total consumer food expenditures, falling from 40.9% to 18.5% in 2006. This has important implications for farm-to-retail price linkages because the smaller the share of farm value in the retail product, the smaller will be the effect of a change in farm price on the retail price.

Economists have identified three fundamental components that define the nature of farm-to-retail price transmission: magnitude (how big is the response at each level to a shock of a given size at another level?); speed of adjustment (are there significant lags in adjustment between marketing levels?); and asymmetry (do adjustments differ depending on whether a shock is transmitted from farm to retail or vice versa?). Price transmission tends to occur both more quickly and more fully for farm commodities that account for a larger share of the final retail product price and that move through more competitive marketing chains.

Economic analysis of farm-to-retail price transmission leads to three generalizations: first, causality usually runs from changes in farm prices to changes in retail prices; second, time lags in retail price response to farm price changes are generally months in length, even for perishables like milk, meat, and fresh fruits and vegetables; and third, retail prices appear to respond asymmetrically, with adjustments to increases in farm prices occurring faster and with greater pass-through than adjustments to decreases in farm prices. This last generalization is often referred to as "sticky" retail food prices—that is, retail prices follow commodity prices upwards rapidly, but fall back only slowly and partially when commodity prices recede. "Sticky" retail price behavior is supported by empirical evidence; however, economic theory does not fully explain the observed phenomenon. Economists have noted that certain aspects of consumer behavior, as well as store inventory management and retailing strategies, may limit retail prices from adjusting fully to downward farm price movements. As a result, the presence of asymmetric price transmission alone does not necessarily imply abnormal or excessive market power.

Comparisons of price data for major food groups confirm that farm-to-retail price transmission behaves slowly, with substantial lags and asymmetry. The rise in farm prices that occurred between 2006 and mid-2008 was substantially larger and occurred about six months earlier than the rise in corresponding retail food product prices. Similarly, the subsequent fall in farm prices from their 2008 peaks preceded the downturn in corresponding retail food prices by several months.

## NOTE TO READERS

This is one of three CRS reports that respond to concerns about the nature and causes of farm and food prices movements. This specific report focuses on the linkages between farm and retail prices. A related report, CRS Report R40545, *Consumers and Food Price Inflation*, provides both background and complementary information for the material presented in this report. It describes how aggregate food price inflation is measured and compares recent price inflation for both at- home (i.e., retail) purchases and away-from-home consumption, as well as by major food groups. An earlier report, CRS Report RL33204, *Price Determination in Agricultural Commodity Markets: A Primer*, describes unique characteristics of market conditions for agricultural products in general, as well as for specific types of agricultural commodities.

## INTRODUCTION

Producers, consumers, and Members of Congress have all expressed strong interest in the connection between farm prices for agricultural commodities and retail prices for food products. Their interest and concerns were heightened in 2008, when prices for many farm commodities rose to record highs in the first half of the year.[1] The higher farm prices quickly worked their way through the marketing system to consumers, where they translated into higher retail food prices— U.S. retail food prices rose an estimated 6.4% in 2008, the largest annual gain since 1990.[2] But the farm price rise was short-lived. Prices for most farm commodities reversed direction in mid-2008 and declined so sharply that they had given back nearly all of their rise by early 2009. In contrast, most retail prices continued to rise until late 2008 or early 2009 before leveling off and/or starting to decline.

These farm and retail price movements were followed closely in the news media,[3] and generated many questions from both interest groups and Congress. What is the relationship between the price of raw agricultural products at the farm and the prices of food products that consumers purchase in retail outlets or at restaurants? Are they subject to the same economic forces? Is there necessarily a lag in retail price response to farm price changes and, if so, what is the nature of that lag? If farm prices rise or fall by a certain percentage, will retail food prices rise or fall by a similar amount, or are retail prices "sticky"— that is, do they tend to follow farm prices up, but not down? What are the principal factors that influence U.S. food prices as commodities move along the marketing chain from producers to consumers? What is the "farm share" of a retail food price and does it matter? What are the primary and secondary data sources for information concerning all of the above issue areas, and how is that information used to help market participants and policymakers make informed decisions?

This report examines the elements contributing to the cost of our food—from the cost of the raw commodity at the farm, through the processing and marketing costs until it is sold to consumers. It also reviews the nature of price transmission between farm and retail prices, and describes how food costs and marketing margins are measured by the government. In particular, it includes a discussion of the evidence concerning "sticky" retail prices (i.e., the idea that retail prices adjust upward quickly when farm prices rise but respond slowly, and possibly not fully, to farm price declines). In a final section, the report uses national average price data to examine farm-to-retail price linkages for several major commodities during the 2006-2009 period, when volatile prices characterized many agricultural markets. In so doing, it attempts to shed light on the evolving structure of U.S. food price formation while providing answers to the above set of questions.

## FOOD: A VALUE-ADDED COMMODITY

When a consumer spends a dollar for food at the supermarket, not all of the dollar reaches the farmer. As the raw ingredients for retail food items move along the marketing chain from the farm to a grain elevator or collection terminal, then on to a processor, a wholesaler, and finally to the retail customer, an array of costs are layered on top of the price of the raw agricultural commodity (**Figure 1**). These marketing costs include labor expenses for handling, sorting, cleaning, and packaging the product, transportation charges to move the product along at each stage, and fees for processing, storing, insuring, financing, and retailing the product (e.g., store maintenance and utilities, refrigeration, labeling, shelf display, advertising and promotional costs).

The farm share of the market price declines as the commodity moves to the retail outlet and consumer. The relative importance of the marketing costs versus raw farm input costs varies widely for different retail food products depending on the degree of processing and transformation. For raw fruits and vegetables, this marketing chain may be significantly shorter than for highly processed products such as a box of breakfast cereal or a ready-to-eat meal.

Marketing costs can also vary by type of retail outlet—for example, farmer's market, big box discount store, local supermarket, in-store deli, 24-hour quick-mart, or ballpark concession stand—as some outlets include substantially more marketing and retailing costs than others.

The U.S. Department of Agriculture's (USDA's) Economic Research Service (ERS) has developed a methodology for monitoring and reporting on the value-added nature of food prices paid by U.S. consumers. Specifically, ERS divides retail prices into two major components:

- the farm-value share, which represents the share that the farmer earns from the retail sale of a food product; and
- the farm-to-retail price spread (also referred to as the marketing margin), which is the difference between a food product's retail price and its farm value.[4]

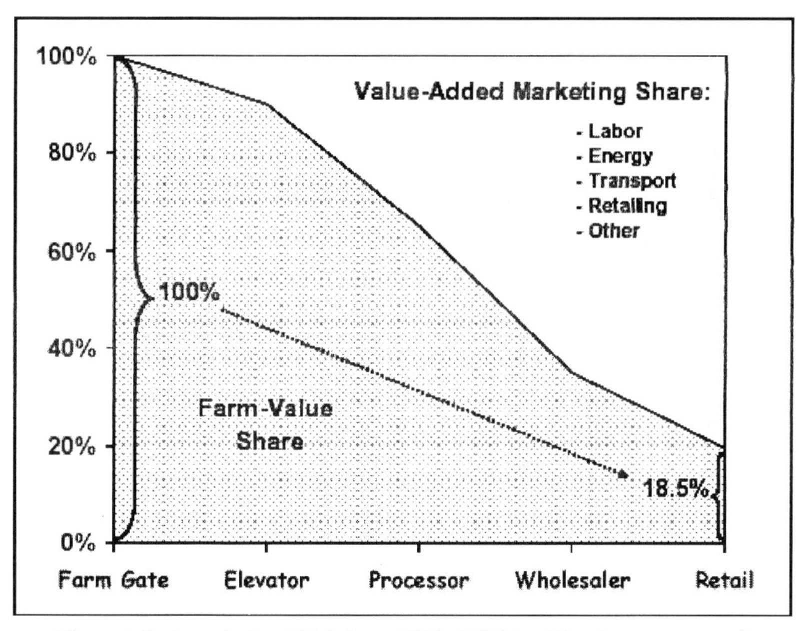


Source: The retail share is for 2006 from ERS, USDA. All other category shares are imputed by CRS.

Figure 1 . Value Added to Farm Products Along the Marketing Chain (average farm-value share of retail food prices as %)

Note that the farm value should not be confused with the farm price. The farm price represents the value at the farm for a unit of agricultural commodity (e.g., a bushel of wheat or a pound of potatoes). In contrast, the farm value of a retail food product is the share of the retail price represented by the amount of raw agricultural commodity needed to produce that retail product. For example, a bushel (60 lbs.) of wheat may cost $4 at the farm, whereas a loaf of bread may cost $1 at the grocery store. The loaf of bread contains substantially less than 60 lbs. of wheat. ERS estimates that a $1 loaf of bread contains about 5¢ worth of wheat.

ERS calculates both the farm-value share and farm-to-retail price spreads for:

- an average "total" food market basket (shown in **Figure 1**, including both at-home and away-from-home purchases);
- nine major food groups (exclusively for at-home consumption, i.e., retail purchases)—meats, poultry, eggs, dairy products, fats and oils, fresh fruits, fresh vegetables, processed fruits and vegetables, and bakery and cereal products; and
- several important individual food items (exclusively for at-home consumption).[5]

The farm-value and the farm-to-retail price spreads provide useful information concerning the potential effect of a farm price change on retail prices, and vice versa. (This is discussed in more detail in the section of this report entitled "Linking Farm and Retail Prices.") They are examined more closely for various food groups in the following four sections.

## Farm-Value Share of Total Consumer Food Purchases

At the most aggregate level, ERS calculates the total U.S. food marketing bill—this is an estimate of the difference between total U.S. consumer food expenditures and the total farm value of domestically grown foods.[6] Total consumer food expenditures (for both at-home and away-fromhome consumption) are calculated by combining retail sales data from the Bureau of Census with the value of food served by schools, hospitals, and other institutions. Imported food and seafood are excluded based on supermarket industry data. ERS calculates the total farm value by multiplying average farm prices from USDA by the quantity of farm products purchased for domestic food use, and then subtracting the value of non-food byproducts. Finally, the resulting difference—the food marketing bill—represents the total U.S. expenditures to transform and deliver domestically produced agricultural products from the farmgate to U.S. consumers as food products.

ERS estimates that total U.S. consumer food expenditures—for both at-home and away-fromhome food—have expanded rapidly from about $110.6 billion in 1970 (**Figure 2**) to nearly $880.7 billion (in nominal dollars) in 2006.[7] However, a substantial portion of the increase in consumer food expenditures has been attributable to general price inflation rather than an increase in the volume of foods purchased. In 1982-1984 dollars, the 2006 total food expenditures bill was $451.2 billion.[8]

During that same period, the marketing bill rose from $75.1 billion to $717.5 billion ($367.6 billion in 1982-1984 dollars, **Figure 3**). In other words, costs for marketing services—such as transportation, processing, and retailing—have grown in both nominal and real terms. In contrast, the farm value of consumer food expenditures has been rising in nominal terms, from $35.5 billion to $163.5 billion, but has been slowly declining in real terms from the mid-1970s to 2006 (from a peak of $107.3 billion to $83.6 billion in 1982-1984 dollars, **Figure 4**).

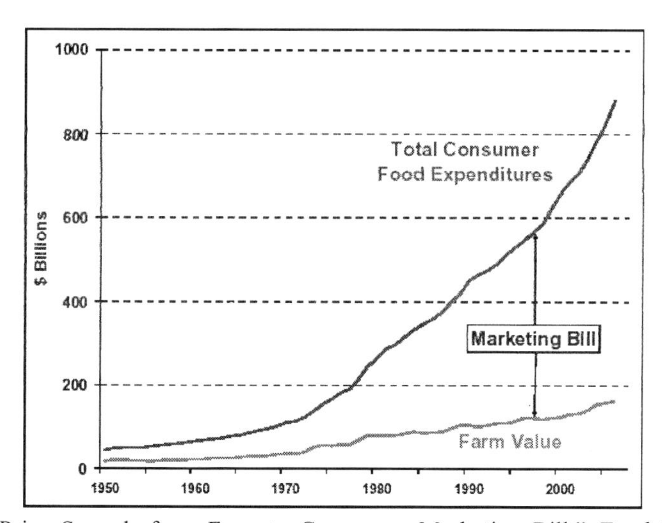


Source: "Price Spreads from Farm to Consumer: Marketing Bill," *Food Marketing System in the U.S.* briefing room, ERS, USDA, at http://www.ers.usda.gov/Data/FarmToConsumer/Data/marketingbilltable1.htm.

Figure 2. Evolution of U.S. Food Expenditures, the Marketing Bill, and the Farm Value of U.S. Foods, 1950-2006

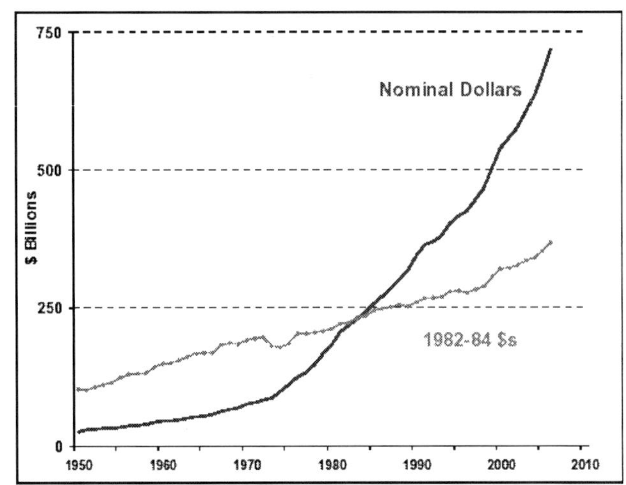


Source: "Price Spreads from Farm to Consumer: Marketing Bill," *Food Marketing System in the U.S.* briefing room, ERS, USDA, at http://www.ers.usda.gov/Data/FarmToConsumer/Data/marketingbilltable1.htm.

Notes: The nominal marketing bill for consumer expenditures of domestically produced farm foods is deflated by the all-item CPI (1982-84 = 100) obtained from the Bureau of Labor Statistics.

Figure 3. U.S. Food Marketing Bill, Real and Nominal, 1950-2006

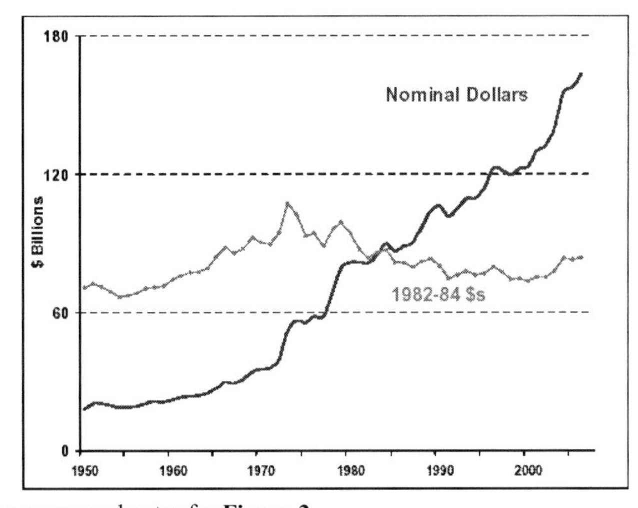


Source: See source and notes for **Figure 3**.

Figure 4. U.S. Farm Value of Total Food Expenditures, Real and Nominal, 1950 to 2006

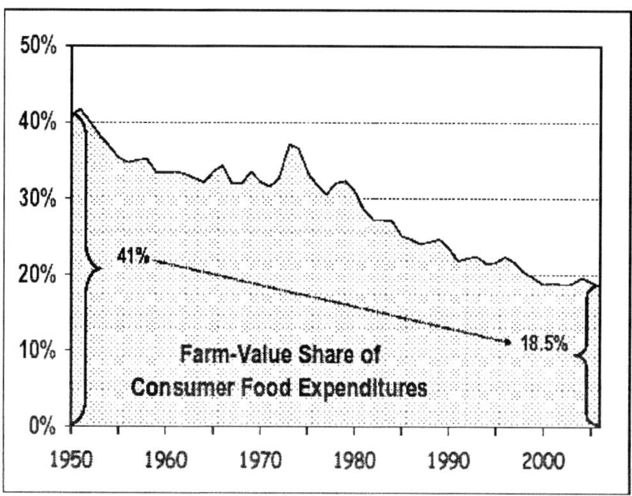


Source: "Price Spreads from Farm to Consumer: Marketing Bill," *Food Marketing System in the U.S.* briefing room, ERS, USDA, at http://www.ers.usda.gov/Data/FarmToConsumer/Data/marketingbilltable1.htm.

Figure 5. Decline of Farm-Value Share as the Food Marketing Bill's Share of U.S. Food Expenditures Has Grown

In addition to a decline in real terms, the farm value of consumer expenditures also has fallen by more than half as a share of consumer food expenditures, falling from a 41% share in 1950 to a 18.5% share in 2006 (**Figure 5**). This means that U.S. farmers have been receiving an increasingly smaller share of what consumers pay for many retail food products over time. However, this should not be misconstrued to suggest that marketing costs are too high, or that farmers' well-being has declined. These statistics do not address either of those issues. Marketing services expand in direct response to consumer demand for more marketing services, which, in turn, occurs for a variety of reasons.[9]

## Farm Share of Retail Food Price Varies by Commodity and Product

In addition to its estimate of total food expenditures (including both at-home and away-from-home expenditures), ERS also constructs food market baskets for consumer at-home expenditures on nine major food subgroupings—meats, poultry, eggs, dairy products, fats and oils, fresh fruits, fresh vegetables, processed fruits and vegetables, and cereal and bakery products—as well as for several important individual food products. ERS then uses the market basket results for the individual foods and groups of food to build an aggregate all-food retail market basket.

These food market baskets contain the average quantities of food from a particular food group purchased by a typical American household during a one-year base period. They include only at-home expenditures on U.S.-produced foods originating on the farm; imports and seafood are excluded, as are away-from-home expenditures. See **Appendix B** of this report for a brief discussion of how the market baskets are derived and then used to estimate the farm-value and marketing bill shares.

**Table 1. Farm-Value Shares for All Foods and Nine Major Food Groups, 2006-2008**

| Food Group[a] | Farm-Value Share[b] | Marketing- Bill Share[c] |
|---|---|---|
| Poultry | 40.8 | 59.2 |
| Eggs | 40.3 | 59.7 |
| Dairy | 32.6 | 67.4 |
| Meat Products | 31.6 | 68.4 |
| Fats & Oils | 22.7 | 77.3 |
| Fresh Vegetables | 19.0 | 81.0 |
| Processed Fruits & Vegetables | 17.0 | 83.0 |
| Fresh Fruit | 16.7 | 83.3 |
| Cereals & Bakery Products | 8.1 | 91.9 |
| **Total Market Basket[d]** | **22.4** | **77.6** |

Source: "Table 8—Farm-Retail Price Spreads," *Agricultural Outlook: Statistical Indicators*, ERS, USDA, available at http://www.ers.usda.gov/publications/agoutlook/aotables/.

Notes: Shares are the three-year average values for 2006-2008 based on the 1982-1983 market basket.

a. Includes foods purchased for at-home consumption only. Farm values for fresh fruits and fresh vegetables are based on prices at first point of sale, and may include marketing charges such as grading and packing for some commodities.

b. The value of the farm input contained in a retail food product, expressed as a share of the retail price.

c. The difference between the retail food product price and the farm-value share.

d. This "total market basket" is limited to at-home expenditures. As a result, it differs from the total farm-value share of 18.5% for 2006 which includes both at-home and away-from-home expenditures.

**Table 2. Average Farm Share of Selected Food Products (Averages for 1998-2000 Period)**

| Food Type | Food Item | Average Farm Share of Retail Price |
|---|---|---|
| Animal products | Eggs, Grade A large, 1 doz. | 50.7 |
| Animal products | Chicken, broiler, 1 lb. | 50.3 |
| Animal products | Beef, choice, 1 lb.** | 48.3 |
| Animal products | Milk, ½ gal. | 38.0 |
| Frozen | Orange juice conc., 12 fl. oz. | 36.0 |
| Animal products | Cheese, natural cheddar, 1 lb. | 33.3 |
| Crop products | Sugar, 1 lb. | 30.0 |
| Dried | Raisins, 15-oz. box | 27.0 |
| Animal products | Pork, 1 lb.** | 27.0 |
| Prepared foods | Peanut butter, 1 lb. | 23.7 |
| Fresh | Fresh—Lemons, 1 lb. | 23.3 |
| Canned and bottled | Canned and bottled—Apple juice, 64-oz. bottle | 23.0 |
| Fresh | Fresh—Lettuce, 1 lb. | 23.0 |
| Canned and bottled | Canned and bottled—Corn, 303 can (17 oz.) | 22.3 |
| Canned and bottled | Canned and bottled—Peas, 303 can (17 oz.) | 22.0 |
| Fresh | Fresh—Oranges, California, 1 lb. | 21.3 |
| Dried | Beans, 1 lb. | 19.7 |
| Fresh | Apples, red delicious, 1 lb. | 19.7 |
| Crop products | Shortening, 3 lbs. | 19.7 |
| Crop products | Margarine, 1 lb. | 19.3 |
| Crop products | Flour, wheat, 5 lbs. | 19.0 |
| Crop products | Rice, long grain, 1 lb. | 18.3 |
| Fresh | Grapefruit, 1 lb. | 17.3 |
| Fresh | Potatoes, 10 lbs. | 17.0 |
| Canned and bottled | Applesauce, 25-oz. jar | 14.7 |
| Canned and bottled | Peaches, cling, 2-1/2 lb. can | 14.3 |
| Canned and bottled | Pears, 2-1/2 lb. can | 14.0 |
| Canned and bottled | Green beans, cut, 303 can (17 oz.) | 13.3 |

**Table 2. (Continued)**

| Food Type | Food Item | Average Farm Share of Retail Price |
|---|---|---|
| Prepared foods | Chicken dinner, fried, frozen, 11 oz. | 13.3 |
| Frozen | Broccoli, cut, 1 lb. | 11.0 |
| Prepared foods | Pork and beans, 303 can (16 oz.) | 11.0 |
| Prepared foods | Potatoes, french-fried, frozen, 1 lb. | 10.7 |
| Prepared foods | Potato chips, regular, 1-lb. bag | 8.3 |
| Frozen | Corn, 1 lb. | 7.7 |
| Canned and bottled | Tomatoes, whole, 303 can (17 oz.) | 7.0 |
| Frozen | Green beans, cut, 1 lb. | 6.0 |
| Prepared foods | Oatmeal regular, 42-oz. box | 5.3 |
| Prepared foods | Bread, 1 lb. | 5.0 |
| Prepared foods | Corn flakes, 18-oz. box | 4.0 |
| Prepared foods | Corn syrup, 16-oz. bottle | 3.0 |

Source: USDA, ERS; calculated by ERS based on data from government and private sources. Available as the "Individual foods" database at http://www.ers.usda.gov/Data/FarmToConsumer/pricespreads.htm.

ERS derives annual estimates of farm-value share and marketing spreads for each of the nine major food groups (**Table 1**) as well as for several individual food items (**Table 2**) based on the respective market baskets. Among these different food products and groupings, the farm-value share varies considerably.

As a rule of thumb, the farmer receives a smaller portion of the shopper's dollar for foods requiring a higher degree of processing or special handling. Among the major food groups, the principal example of this is "cereals and bakery products," where the farm-value share was just 8.1% during the 2006-2008 period. Cereals and bakery products involve a substantial degree of processing, first through a flour mill, then through a food processing plant, where the grain flour is combined with other products and baked before being packaged and shipped off to retail outlets. In addition, substantial costs are involved in shipping bakery products (e.g., each item is individually shelved so as not to crush ready-to-eat products). Finally, most cereal and bakery products are subject to substantial advertising and retailing costs, as competition for consumer interests can be fierce. This contrasts with poultry and egg products, whose average farm-value shares were both estimated to be above 40% during 2006-2008.

The low farm-value shares for fresh fruits (16.7% in **Table 1**) and vegetables (19%) suggests that, as perishable fresh products are shipped greater distances, handling and sorting, shelving and crating, refrigeration, shipping, and labeling have become increasingly important components of retail prices. However, ERS research has shown that the fresh fruit and vegetable farm-value share is particularly susceptible to understatement due to the inflexible calculation method adopted by ERS.[10]

**Table 2** presents ERS calculations of the farm-value share for several individual food items. The rule of thumb mentioned earlier clearly holds—the more highly processed food items have significantly lower farm-value shares than less processed products.

## The Marketing Bill

By definition, the difference between the retail price of a food product and its farm value is the marketing bill (referred to earlier as the farm-to-retail price spread or marketing margin). As such it includes all costs associated with getting the raw commodity from the farm to the consumer (including any profits).

The size of the marketing bill is affected by changes in the amount and type of products consumers buy.[11] For example, restaurant meals have more marketing costs associated with them, and are therefore more expensive than foods at grocery stores. So, as consumers spend more of their food budget at restaurants, the marketing bill increases. Similarly, as consumers purchase more highly processed food products, such as microwave-ready dinners, relative to less processed fruits, vegetables, and meats, the marketing bill increases. Also, as food products travel greater distances to reach consumers, their marketing bill increases. Since 1950, the U.S. marketing bill has increasingly taken a larger share of the consumer food dollar, growing from 59.1% of consumer food spending to 81.5% in 2006 (**Figure 5**).

In 2006, USDA estimated that the average farm-value share of all food products of U.S. farm- origin consumed in the United States (both at-home and away-from-home) was 18.5% (**Figure 6**) out of an estimated $880.7 billion. The other 81.5% covered the cost of transforming the raw U.S. farm commodities into food products and getting them to the retail store shelves, restaurants, and other consumer outlets.

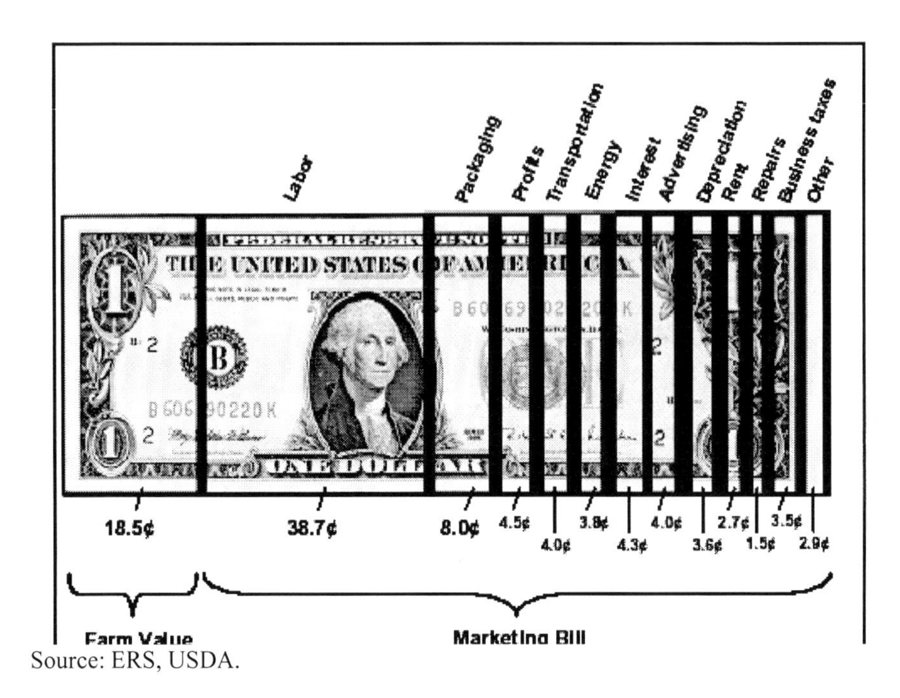


Source: ERS, USDA.

Figure 6. What a Dollar Spent on Food Paid for in 2006

Besides showing how much the marketing system as a whole receives, the national marketing bill provides a good indication of how these expenditures are divided among such marketing inputs as labor, energy, profits, transportation, and so forth. Moreover, it enables ERS analysts to measure annual changes in the individual components of the total marketing bill. ERS estimates 11 cost components of the marketing bill, as listed in **Figure 6**.[12] These major components (and their respective marketing-bill shares) are briefly listed below.

- **Labor** (38.7%) is the single largest cost in the marketing bill. Labor costs include wages and salaries of employees (e.g., meat cutters in the slaughterhouse, grocery clerks, and store managers); imputed earnings of proprietors, active partners, and unpaid family workers in retail stores and away-from-home eating places; and supplements to wages and salaries such as pensions and health insurance.

- **Packaging** (8%) is the second-largest component of the marketing bill and represents 8¢ of every dollar spent on a consumer food item. Packaging material costs include the cost of paper products, and metal, glass, plastic, and wooden containers. Firms that process and distribute foods purchase nearly half of all containers and packaging materials used in the United States.

- **Profits** (4.5%) are ERS estimates of pre-tax profits earned by corporations for manufacturing, wholesaling, and retailing U.S.-produced farm foods.

- **Transportation** (4%) represents the costs associated with moving farm output along the marketing chain to the consumer, including both truck and inter-city rail movements. Costs specifically include fuel, drivers' wages, and other related charges.

- **Energy** costs (3.8%) include only the costs of electricity, natural gas, and other fuels used in food processing, wholesaling, retailing, and food-service establishments. Transportation fuel costs are counted separately.

- **Interest** costs (4.3%), net of any interest income, are related to financing charges.

- **Advertising** costs (4.0%) include expenditures for television, radio, and newspaper advertising. In 2006, nearly $35 billion was spent on food advertising costs in the United States, suggesting a high degree of competition for consumer dollars.

- **Depreciation** (3.6%) is an allowance for the decline in value of capital assets caused by obsolescence and physical deterioration of buildings and equipment.

- **Rent** expenses (2.7%), net of any rent income, are charges on any of the capital assets used in retailing food products.

- **Repair** costs (1.5%) are expenditures for maintenance and incidental repairs and costs of labor, supplies, and other items that do not add to the value or appreciably prolong the life of a capital asset.

- **Business taxes** (3.5%) include property, state, unemployment insurance, and social security taxes but not federal income taxes.

- **Other** costs (2.9%) are a miscellaneous collection of expenses that do not fit into any of the above categories. On average, they account for about 2.9¢ of every consumer food dollar.

ERS calculates labor costs using payroll data from the Bureau of the Census and the Bureau of Labor Statistics. Packaging and energy costs are calculated from Census data. The remaining cost components are derived from Internal Revenue Service statistics.

## LINKING FARM AND RETAIL PRICES

Price is the primary mechanism by which various levels of the market system are linked. While farmers and consumers sometimes do meet directly in farmers' markets, in most cases the raw farm product is separated from the retail food product by a complex processing and distribution system.[13] Farm-to-retail price changes may originate from three potential sources: (1) changes in farm prices; (2) changes in prices of marketing inputs along the farm-to-retail marketing chain; or (3) changes in retail prices. This section will briefly discuss the various factors involved in understanding farm-to-retail price linkages—in particular, how they are measured and what influences them.

### Farm-to-Retail Marketing Margin

As defined earlier, the farm-to-retail price spread is the difference between the farm-value share (i.e., the portion received by producers) of a food product's price and the price paid by final consumers. To estimate a food product's farm-to-retail price spread, the farm-value share must first be calculated. Once the farm-value share of a retail price is determined, then the price spread itself is determined. As a result, the Economic Research Service (ERS) reports both farm-value shares and price spreads together.[14] Price spreads may be calculated at various stages along the market chain as, for example, the farm-to-wholesale margin, the wholesale-to-retail margin, and the farm-to-retail margin.

## Measuring Farm-to-Retail Price Linkages

Farm and retail prices are linked by the evolving dynamic embodied in the marketing system's attempt to respond to consumers' demand for marketing services. Changes in consumer preferences for food products at the retail level (e.g., increased demand for consumer-ready food products) can drive the food marketing system to add more or fewer services to the commodities grown by farmers. As the mix and price of services required to transform raw agricultural commodities into consumer food products changes, so too does a food product's farm-value share and farm-to-retail price spread.[15]

As a result, the nature of price transmission between the price paid by the consumer for the retail food product and the farm price of the underlying agricultural commodity can be better understood by evaluating two key aspects of any particular food product: (1) the farm-value share of the retail price, and (2) the competitiveness of markets at each stage of the marketing chain.

### *Farm-Value Share*

The larger the share of farm value in the retail product, the greater will be the effect of a change in farm price, other things being equal. In direct contrast, the greater the degree and duration of processing and value-added that is accumulated between the farm and the consumers, the smaller will be the effect of a change in farm price on the retail price. In other words, more highly processed food products are likely to show less price response to a change in the related farm commodity price than are less-processed retail products like meat. (However, some factors affecting farm commodity prices, e.g., energy costs, may concomitantly affect marketing inputs and services, which, in turn, would impact retail prices.)

The share of marketing inputs and services embodied in retail food products has been growing steadily over time relative to the farm-value share, as shown earlier (**Figure 2**). This would suggest that retail price responsiveness to farm price changes has been gradually diminishing over time.

### *Market Competition*

Price transmission will tend to occur both more quickly and more fully to changes in market conditions for farm commodities that move through marketing chains subject to more highly competitive market conditions—that is, markets with a large number of buyers and sellers dealing in commodities that have several potential close substitutes and where market information is transparent and easily accessed by all participants—than for those subject to less competitive market conditions.[16] In uncompetitive markets, certain participants may wield an abnormal degree of market power and, as a result, prices may be less responsive to changes in market conditions.

The growing concentration of processing and retail firms in many food product markets has led many to question whether certain market participants wield excessive market power and exert undue influence in price formation. This concern has attracted greater scrutiny to changing market structures within the U.S. food distribution network, and their potential effect on farm-to-retail price linkages. However, several factors other than market power can also make measuring the farm-to-retail price spread a difficult exercise.

### *Potential Measurement Difficulties*

First is the fact that many agricultural commodities are used for numerous final products. Take corn, for example. Corn's primary use is as an energy source in animal feed rations. However, corn is also processed into a large number of food and industrial products, including corn oil, starch, high fructose corn syrup, corn flour, grits, corn meal, beverage alcohols, and ethanol. The demand for corn at the farm level is derived from the demand for each of these uses, each of which trades in its own market subject to its own set of economic conditions. The same is true for soybeans, sorghum, wheat, and most other raw agricultural commodities.

In other words, U.S. and international consumers must compete with livestock and poultry feeding operations, and industrial and other types of non-food uses, for a portion of U.S. agricultural output. The portion of non-food uses has expanded rapidly in recent years with the emergence of agriculture-based biofuel production as a new source of demand for raw agricultural commodities. These multiple sources of demand weaken the price linkage between the price for any single retail product and its related farm commodity price.

Another emerging factor that weakens the direct farm-to-retail price linkage is the evolution of the U.S. food distribution network, which has experienced a substantial expansion in the number and type of outlets in recent decades. This includes the growth of big box discount stores, the integration of ready-to-eat foods and/or deli sections at grocery stores, mini-marts, gas stations, pharmacies, and other non-traditional outlets, and online food delivery services. As a result of this dynamic evolution in commodity markets and food retailing, simple pricing structures have increased in complexity and the link between farmers and consumers is gradually becoming more diffuse, especially for highly processed products.

A prime example of this is how, in response to changing consumer preferences, grocery stores have been expanding consumer convenience by offering prepared entrees and side dishes ready for the oven, microwave, or even the dinner table. Many grocery store chains now include ready-to-eat food buffets and deli sections where made-to-take meals are prepared. All of these transformations are increasing the share of services needed to convert agricultural commodities into retail food products. This lowers the farm-value share of retail prices and weakens the potential retail price response to a change in a farm commodity price.

## Farm-to-Retail Price Transmission

Vertical price transmission (hereafter referred to simply as price transmission) is the process by which changes in farm prices are transmitted along the marketing chain both downstream from farm to retail and upstream from retail to farm.[17] The adjustment to price shocks along the marketing chain is an important characteristic of the functioning of markets.

Economists have identified three fundamental components that define the nature of price transmission:[18]

- **Magnitude.** How big is the response at each level to a shock of a given size at another level? This is referred to as the extent of pass-through. For example, a 100% pass-through from farm to retail would imply equal percent price changes at both the retail and farm level.

- **Speed of adjustment.** Are there significant lags in adjustment between marketing levels?

- **Asymmetry.** Do adjustments differ depending on whether a shock is transmitted downwards (from farm to retail) or upwards (from retail to farm) along the marketing chain?

Asymmetry in price transmission directly encapsulates the concept of "sticky" retail prices mentioned earlier and addressed later in this report. To better understand asymmetric price transmission, consider two hypothetical examples (**Figure 7** and **Figure 8**) where a price rise at the farm level transmits both faster and more fully to the retail level than does a price decline. In the first scenario (**Figure 7**), an upward farm price shock of 40% occurs immediately at the start of the first month (M1). The farm price shock translates into a gradual 15% retail price rise that begins one month later and is spread over an entire month. In this case the magnitude or degree of pass-through would be (15%)/(40%) = 37.5% with a two-month lag.

In contrast, the second example (**Figure 8**) is of a downward farm price shock of 50% that eventually transmits into a 10% decline in retail prices. The retail price decline begins three months after the initial farm price shock, and is extended over a three-month period for the 10% retail decline to fully occur. Most of the pass-through occurs during the fourth and fifth months, followed by a very gradual sixth month of decline. In this later example, the magnitude of pass- through is (10%)/(50%) = 20% with a six-month lag.

The implication of asymmetric price transmission as portrayed by these examples is that consumers at the retail level would not fully benefit from a price reduction at the farm level. In contrast, processors and retailers would likely benefit from such "sticky" retail prices. One could also envision a case where an upward shock to retail prices due to a surge in consumer demand is only partially passed through to farm prices such that producers would not fully benefit from the retail price increase.

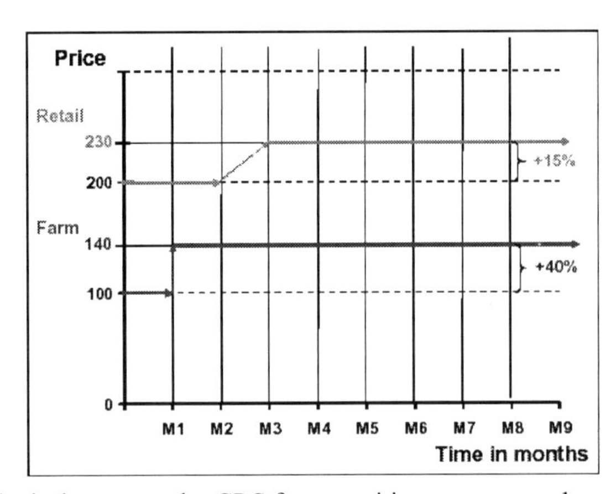


Source: Hypothetical construct by CRS for exposition purposes only.

Note: In this example, the farm price rise occurs immediately at the start of the first month, and is 40% of the initial farm price of 100. In contrast , the rise in the associated retail price begins one month later and takes one month to occur. When fully expressed, the retail price rise is 15% above the initial 200.

Figure 7. Hypothetical Price Transmission Following an Upward Farm Price Shock

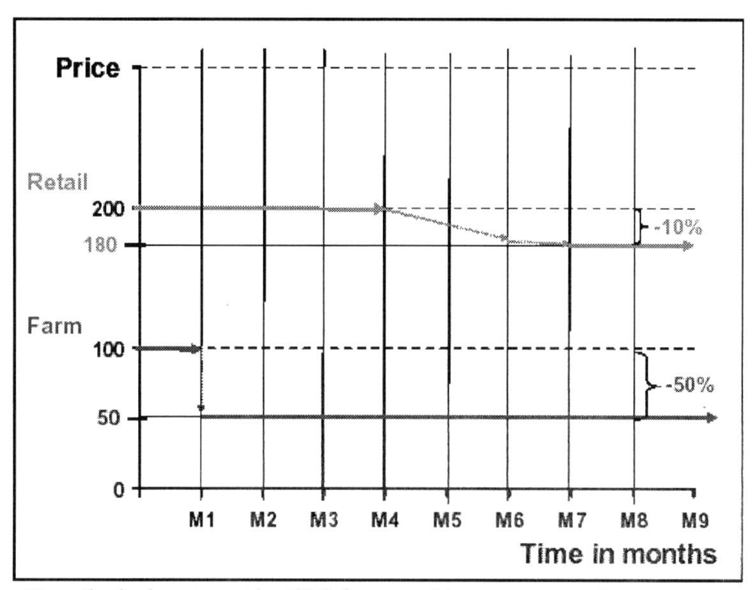


Source: Hypothetical construct by CRS for exposition purposes only.

Note: In this example, the farm price decline occurs immediately and is roughly 50% of the initial price (100). In contrast , the decline in the associated retail price starts three months later and is spread over a three-month period, with most of the transmission taking place during the fourth and fifth months following the initial shock. When fully expressed, the full retail price decline is roughly 10% of the initial retail price of 200.

Figure 8. Hypothetical Price Transmission Following a Downward Farm Price Shock

Agricultural producer groups are often annoyed when farm prices fall by more than retail prices, but economic analysis has shown that this can occur in a competitive market.[19] In other words, abnormal market power (e.g., monopoly, oligopoly, monopsony) need not be present for the phenomenon of asymmetric or "sticky" retail prices to exist. This is discussed further in the section of this report entitled "Why Do Retail Prices Tend to Be Sticky?"

### *What Is Known about Price Transmission?*

While much empirical evidence exists in support of asymmetry between farm and retail prices, the empirical analysis is still inconclusive concerning the specific nature of price pass-through between farm and retail markets.[20] This is perhaps largely because agricultural markets in general encompass such a vast array of commodities and products—each with their own particular set of product characteristics and market conditions. However, a broad review of economic analysis on the relationship between farm and retail prices leads to three generalizations:[21]

- first, causality usually runs from changes in farm prices to changes in retail prices;
- second, time lags in retail price response to farm price changes are generally months in length, even for perishables like milk, meat, and fresh fruits and vegetables; and
- third, retail prices appear to respond asymmetrically, with adjustments to increases in farm prices occurring faster and with greater pass-through than adjustments to decreases in farm prices.

### *Why Do Retail Prices Tend to Be Sticky?*

The general perception (supported by considerable empirical evidence) is that retail food prices are "sticky"—that is, retail prices follow commodity prices upwards rapidly, but fall back only slowly and partially when commodity prices recede. A common concern of policymakers is that this retail "stickiness" is due to imperfect price transmission perceived to be caused by market power and oligopolistic behavior at some stage of the marketing chain.[22]

According to economic theory, the "stickiness" of retail prices should be inversely related to the degree of retail competition in a locality. More retail shopping opportunities in close proximity would engender greater price competition and should diminish the "stickiness" of retail prices. The same would be true of wholesale prices and markets, or any other stage of the marketing chain. However, economic theory does not fully explain the observed phenomena.

Economists have noted several exceptions to the "retail price competition" paradigm that may limit retail prices from adjusting fully to downward farm price movements, including certain aspects of consumer behavior, as well as store inventory management and retailing strategies. As a result, the presence of asymmetric price transmission alone does not necessarily imply the presence of excessive market power. This section briefly discusses some of the various factors that might produce asymmetric price transmission other than market power.

### Consumer Behavior

First, consider how consumer behavior could encourage price stickiness. Consumers often must make their food purchases while considering tight budget constraints. However, several factors other than retail price may enter into their grocery purchase decision, including time and convenience of food acquisition, strong consumer store preference, or strongly established consumer shopping patterns (e.g., picking up groceries at the nearby store on the way home from work). Also, the average level of a consumer's wealth is important, since higher-income consumers tend to be less price-conscious and less likely to change stores or shopping patterns due to food price changes. All of these factors contribute to a lower price responsiveness by consumers to retail price changes, which, in turn, allows retail outlets to keep prices higher than they otherwise would (were consumers more price-responsive) without losing market share, revenues, or profits.

### Search Cost

Retail prices are local in the sense that consumers do not venture far to buy milk and fresh produce for daily consumption. When retail prices for certain food products rise, consumers may be reluctant to invest the necessary time to find cheaper alternatives. This concept is referred to as "search cost" by economists. A consumer will accept a "higher" retail price if the cost to change shopping patterns and search out a better price is perceived as exceeding the potential savings from such an act, particularly when the consumer would have to balance the savings for any one item obtained by switching grocery stores against possible price losses on other retail products in the new store.

### Retail Inventory Management

Retail inventory management could also contribute to sticky prices. Large retail inventories purchased or forward-contracted during a period of high commodity prices may limit a shopkeeper's ability to lower prices. This would depend on how much profit margin exists on each item and how much loss on each item a store is willing or able to absorb. As a result of such inventory management issues, there is often a substantial time lag between farm and retail price changes—a decline in farm prices may take several months to pass through to retail stores as retail stores work through higher-priced inventories and contractual purchase obligations.

### Menu Cost

The cost to a retail store of lowering prices may be prohibitive. Referred to in economic jargon as *menu cost*, this refers to the costs associated with making changes in retail prices such as remarking in-store price labels, updating advertisements and promotional flyers, and the like. Also associated with menu cost is the risk to the retailer's reputation from frequent price changes that send complex signals to shoppers. A retail store's perception of menu cost and its influence is also related to consumers' price responsiveness for a particular food item. For example, if the increase in sales generated by the lower price would fail to offset the cost associated with re-marking price labels, then a retail store would likely not lower its prices.

### Market Uncertainty

Market price uncertainty regarding whether a price shock is permanent or temporary may influence retail price strategy, as firms are generally reluctant to chase temporary price movements. Such uncertainty may contribute to asymmetry in retail and farm price movements. For example, during periods when commodity and energy prices are particularly volatile (as in 2008), retailers may be reluctant to lower prices if there is a significant probability that their costs may turn around and rise quickly thereafter.

Volatile commodity prices generally translate into higher retail prices as dealers try to lock in profit margins in the face of uncertain costs. Subsequent "sticky" retail prices mean that consumers benefit only partially when commodity prices recede and are left with the perception (if not the reality) of paying for higher retail profit margins. In contrast, farm prices respond quickly to market conditions because most agricultural markets are highly competitive and because, unlike retailers, farmers have little say in the price at which they sell their products, only in the timing of such sales.

#### *Incidence of a Change in Marketing Costs*

In addition to the timing and pass-through aspects of price transmission, policy makers and market participants have also expressed concern over the incidence of an increase in the price of an input to the retail food production process (such as an increase in energy costs). Who bears the added cost? Is it passed on to consumers in the form of higher prices, or to farmers in the form of lower prices, or is it absorbed by food processors in the form of lower revenues? Most economists would agree that the time period under consideration is critical when evaluating the incidence of a change in a marketing input cost.

Economic theory suggests that the price of the average food product will be more sensitive to an input price change in the short run than in the long run due to the time needed for price-induced behavioral adjustments to occur. For some commodities there may be a substantial time lag for food processors and consumers to adjust their behavior in response to a change in retail prices that result from a change in the price of a retail food product input (whether it originates from the farm component or the non-farm marketing component)—whether an input purchase or technology adjustment in the case of food processors; or an adjustment to inventories held by wholesalers or retailers; or a different consumption choice in the case of a consumer.

In the long run, both firms (food producers) and consumers have more time to adjust their behavior to relative input price changes, thereby mitigating the effects on consumer food prices.

Some firms may exit the industry, while others may adjust their input mix by finding a cheaper alternative input or by altering the food processing technology so as to use less of the more expensive input or perhaps switch to a different input entirely. Finally, some firms seek out increased supplies of the more expensive input via imports or expanded domestic production (which would require a new growing cycle).

Similarly, in the long run, consumers have more time to substitute among food products in favor of obtaining their nutritional needs at the lowest cost. In so doing they shift their demand among individual food products.

In the short run, the time period is sufficiently short that wholesalers and retailers are unable to adjust their behavior or their technology or to acquire additional lower-cost supplies of the relevant marketing input. Then, food producers and consumers are limited in their response to an unexpected input price change. Under these conditions, a larger portion of an input price increase is usually passed along to consumers in the form of higher retail prices.

### *Extenuating Circumstances for Farm-to-Food Price Linkages*

Certain characteristics of individual farm commodities can play an important role in determining the price transmission between the farm and the retail consumer. For example, livestock production tends to have a cyclical pattern driven by biological constraints in the gestation-birth process that limit producer response to market conditions. As a result, meat and dairy product prices are influenced by the long lag time involved in industry adjustments to input (feed costs) or output price changes.

Annual crops tend to have seasonal patterns, although this pattern is strongly influenced by the storability of the individual commodity. Perishable products have shorter shelf-life and often require greater handling. As a result, prices for perishable products tend to show strong seasonal patterns; they are vulnerable to volatile swings as near-term conditions change; and long-term price formation is less correlated with current supplies and more correlated with producer behavior. In contrast, storable commodities (e.g., grains) can be moved in bulk and stored for several years at a time such that current supplies are an important factor in determining price volatility as well as both current and long-term price formation.

On the demand side, many food products have strong seasonal patterns of demand. For example, meat demand tends to rise in the summer months when grilling activity is at a maximum, and the demand for turkey is strongly correlated with the Thanksgiving and Christmas holidays.

## FARM AND RETAIL PRICES COMPARED

During the 2006 to 2009 period, the news media has reported on unusually wide variances between low farm and high retail prices, suggesting that perhaps some food retailers were profiting unfairly by engaging in price gouging.[23] The retail grocery business is highly competitive, making it unlikely that such activity could occur either on a large scale or for a sustained period of time. Sometimes consumers tend to focus on a single highly visible item that is purchased routinely (such as milk) to draw their conclusions about retail price responsiveness and market power, without fully understanding the time lag involved in a farm-to-retail price response for most commodities.

Another retail marketing consideration that may cloud retail price perceptions by consumers (about whether asymmetric price transmission has occurred) is the use of "loss leader" items, whereby a retail outlet sets the price for highly visible consumer items at below cost as a marketing strategy to attract consumers into the store. Supplementary consumer purchases of other goods with normal retail markups would then offset the loss on the leader items. Consumers may be easily confused when neighboring stores use different products as loss leaders, particularly in a period of volatile prices.

This final section uses national average price data to examine the farm-to-retail price linkages for several major commodities during the 2006 to 2009 period, when volatile prices characterized many agricultural markets. Price indexes for major food groups are presented in a series of graphs to allow for a visual comparison of farm, wholesale (when available), and retail price movements for differences in magnitude, timing, and asymmetry in adjustment. This section is followed (in **Appendix A**) by a series of comparisons of actual price data for certain select retail food products and their corresponding agricultural commodities.

## Aggregate Price Indexes

In 2008, retail food prices rose by an average of 5.5%, the largest percentage increase since 1989. This increase is extremely modest when compared to the price rise during the first half of the year for most farm commodities. However, to fully capture the potential time lags in price response between the relative rise in farm and retail prices, a longer historical perspective is preferable. Since the rise in farm prices began in mid-2006, that year is selected as the reference base.

A comparison of national aggregate indexes for farm (monthly average farm price received, or MAFP, for food commodities), wholesale (Producer Price Index or PPI for finished consumer foods), and retail (Consumer Price Index or CPI for food-at-home purchases), indicates that average farm prices rose 33.2% from the 2006 base (i.e., 2006 = 100) to its peak in July 2008 (**Figure 9**). Wholesale food prices rose 15.8% to their peak in September 2008 (two months later), and retail food prices rose 13.8% to a peak in January 2009 (six months after the farm price peak). The percent rise in farm commodity prices was more than double the percent rise in either wholesale or retail prices.

Now consider how far farm and retail prices have fallen from their peaks. Aggregate farm-product prices fell nearly 22% from their July 2008 peak until their trough eight months later in March 2009. Wholesale prices fell slightly over 4% from their peak in September 2008 until their bottom (six months later) in March 2009. By April 2009, retail prices had dropped about 2% from their January 2009 peak, but were still trending lower. If retail prices hit their trough with the same lag to farm prices as their peak (i.e., six months), then they can be expected to bottom out in September 2009. This cursory examination of national aggregate indexes suggests that it is wholesale prices (at the food processor level) that have adjusted only minimally to farm-level price declines. However, it is possible that wholesale prices may still resume their downward adjustment in 2009. As for retail prices, which are still in a downward adjustment phase, only time will tell how fully retail prices will ultimately adjust.

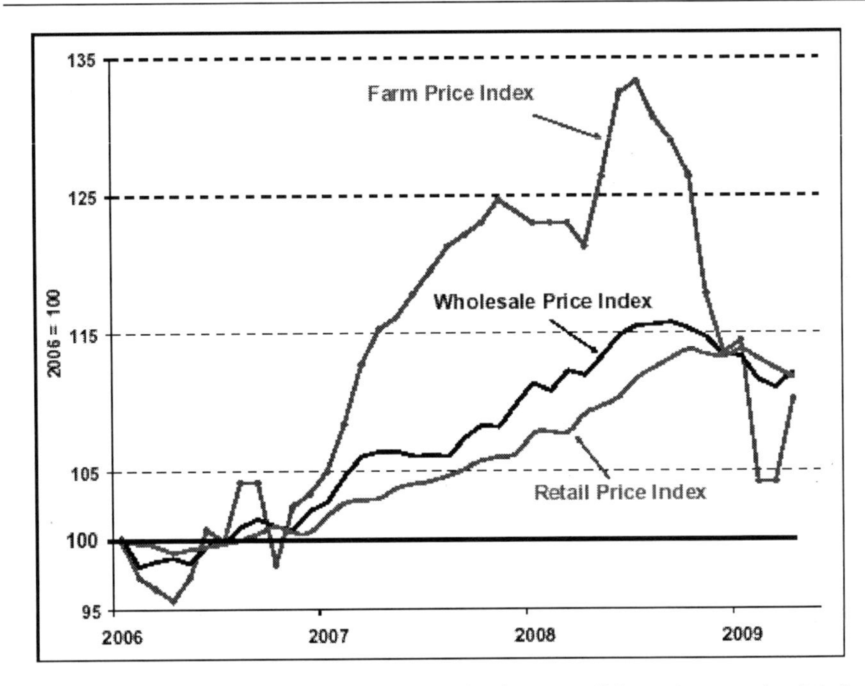


Source: The Farm Price Index is the farm food commodities prices-received index from the National Agricultural Statistics Service (NASS), USDA; the Retail Price Index is the Food-at-Home CPI from the Bureau of Labor Statistics (BLS); and the Wholesale Price index is the Producer Price Index (PPI) for Finished Consumer Foods from BLS.

Figure 9. Price Indexes for Farm, Wholesale, and Retail Food Products, 2006-2009

### *Grocer Margins*

The spread between the food-at-home CPI (reflecting retail prices) and the PPI for finished consumer foods (reflecting wholesale prices) is often studied by market analysts as a gauge for grocer margins.[24] Clearly, by this comparison, the first three months of 2009 (**Figure 9**), when the CPI exceeded the PPI, represented a period of profitable margins for grocers (as did the first half of 2006).

Of course, retail price changes vary widely by specific commodity and market. In addition, it is likely that retail prices will continue to decline in early 2009, as farm-to-retail price transmission can often entail a substantial time lag of a several months.

Grocery store sales are generally competitive and, as a result, most prices stay within a fairly narrow trading range to avoid altering consumer behavior.

In addition, the value added by the food marketing system is largely independent of farm prices, as evidenced when consumer prices have held steady or risen in the face of a decline in farm prices.[25]

### *Declining Real Farm Prices*

Historically farm prices have been subject to significant downward pressure due to tremendous gains in agricultural productivity. Improvements in farm machinery, cultivation and conservation practices, fertilizers and pesticides, animal husbandry, and animal and plant genetics have all contributed to significant productivity gains in U.S. agricultural production, which in turn have resulted in agricultural output tending to expand faster than demand. As a result, farm prices have been declining in real terms steadily since the late 1940s, as exemplified by the farm price of corn (**Figure 10**).

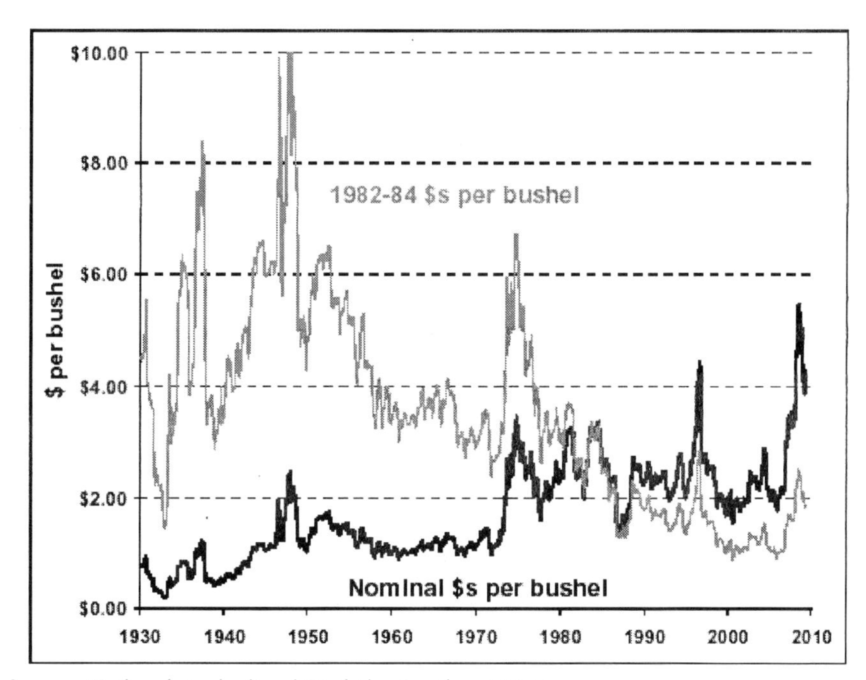


Source: National Agricultural Statistics Service, USDA.

Notes: The nominal farm price is deflated by the all-item CPI (1982-1984 = 100) obtained from the Bureau of Labor Statistics.

Figure 10. U.S. Monthly Farm Price for Corn, 1930-2009

**Table 3. Farm, Wholesale, and Retail Price Movements, 2006 to 2009**

| Corresponding Figure | Commodity or Food Group | Market Level | % Change: 2006-to-Peak[a] | % Change: Peak-to-2009[b] |
|---|---|---|---|---|
| Figure 9 | MAFP[c] Index: All Food Commodities | Farm | 33.2% | -21.8% |
| | PPI:[d] Finished Consumer Foods | Wholesale | 15.8% | -4.1% |
| | CPI:[e] Food-at-Home | Retail | 13.8% | -1.8% |
| Figure 11 | MAFP Index: food grains | Farm | 128.5% | -34.6% |
| | CPI: cereals & bakery products | Retail | 19.5% | -0.7% |
| Figure 12 | MAFP Index; eggs | Farm | 134.0% | -41.4% |
| | CPI: eggs | Retail | 58.8% | -17.7% |
| Figures 13 & 14 | MAFP Index; dairy products | Farm | 33.2% | -21.8% |
| | PPI: fluid milk | Wholesale | 69.5% | -47.5% |
| Figure 13 | CPI: fresh milk | Retail | 24.1% | -19.5% |
| Figure 14 | CPI: cheese | Retail | 23.0% | -8.1% |
| Figure 15 | MAFP Index; broilers | Farm | 38.6% | -10.0% |
| | PPI: slaughter chicken | Wholesale | 48.8% | -15.9% |
| | CPI: poultry | Retail | 13.0% | -0.2% |
| Figure 16 | MAFP Index: all beef, 500+ lbs. | Farm | 10.3% | -18.0% |
| | PPI: slaughter cattle | Wholesale | 17.3% | -20.0% |
| | CPI: beef | Retail | 13.5% | -3.8% |
| Figure 17 | MAFP Index: barrows & gilts | Farm | 31.4% | -33.4% |
| | PPI: slaughter hogs | Wholesale | 38.9% | -35.1% |
| | CPI: pork | Retail | 8.7% | -5.6% |

Source: Calculated by CRS from the source data identified in each of the figures cited in the table.

Note: The price data are adjusted such that average prices for the year 2006 = 100.

a. Peak value was selected as the highest value that occurred during the 2007 to 2009 period.

b. Percent change from peak value to lowest value point in 2009 (through April of 2009).

c. MAFP = Monthly Average Farm Price received as reported by NASS, USDA.

d. PPI = Producer Price Index as reported by the Bureau of Labor Statistics (BLS).

e. CPI = Consumer Price Index as reported by BLS.

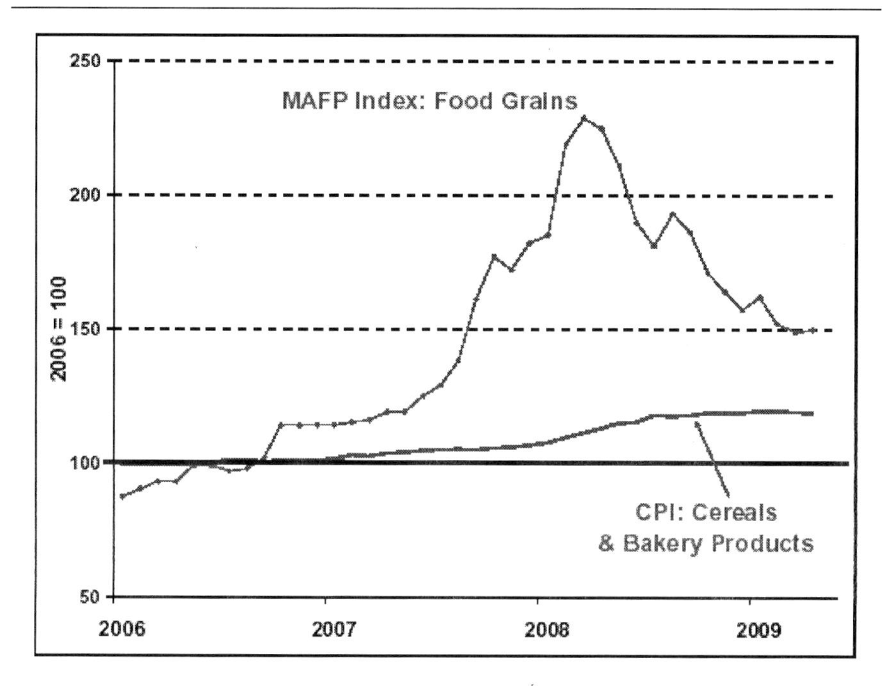


Source: Monthly average farm prices (MAFP) received are from NASS, USDA; Consumer Price Indexes (CPI) for major retail food groups are from the Bureau of Labor Statistics (BLS).

Figure 11. Cereal Price Indexes: Farm Food Grains vs. Retail Cereals and Bakery Products

In contrast, the marketing bill has been subject to general inflationary pressures despite certain technological gains (e.g., in the processing, storage, and transportation sectors). As a result, the food marketing bill has risen rapidly in nominal dollars, and slowly but steadily in real terms (**Figure 3**). As a result, the farm share has tended to decline for most foods, while farm-to-consumer price spreads have widened. This is indicative of the extent to which the components of general inflation (i.e., energy, labor, rental rates, etc.) have increased in importance as a share of retail food prices.

## Price Indexes for Major Food Groups

This section uses a series of charts (**Figure 11** to **Figure 17**) and a table (**Table 3**) to compare price indexes for farm and retail prices for several major food groups. The corresponding wholesale price index is included when available. The monthly average farm price (MAFP)-received data represent national averages that have been adjusted to comparable indexes where the average price for the year 2006 = 100. This allows a pure comparison across all prices indexes—farm (MAFP), wholesale (PPI), and retail (food-at-home CPI)—relative to their 2006 base. As mentioned earlier, most agricultural prices began their rise in 2006, making it an obvious point of comparison.

Readers should note that, in every case, the farm and wholesale price movements are substantially larger than the corresponding retail price movements over the 2006-2009 period. Also, in all of the following price index charts, the retail price peak follows the farm price peak with a lag of one to two months, with the exception of egg prices, where the farm and retail price indexes peaked in the same month, and cereal and bakery products, which peaked several months later than the farm price.

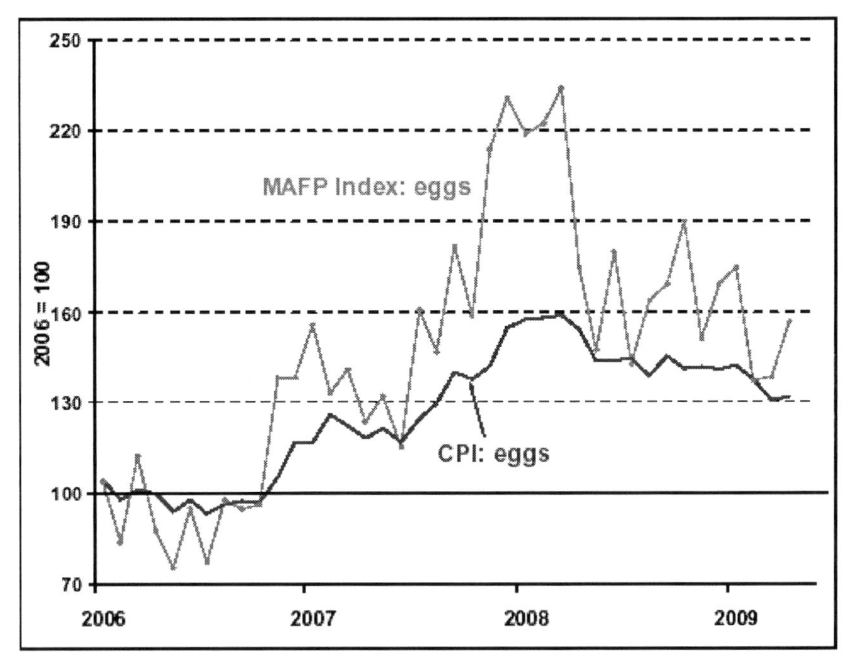


Source: Monthly average farm prices (MAFP) received are from NASS, USDA; Producer Price Index (PPI) and Consumer Price Indexes (CPI) for major retail food groups are from BLS.

Figure 12. Egg Price Indexes: Farm Prices Received vs. Retail Price

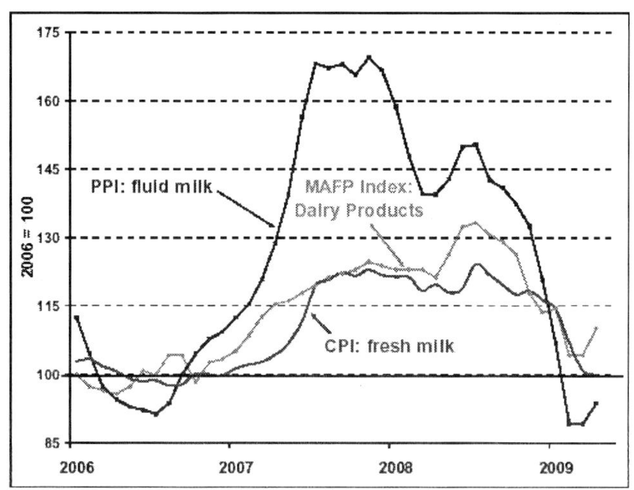


Source: Monthly average farm prices (MAFP) received are from NASS, USDA; Producer Price Index (PPI) and Consumer Price Indexes (CPI) for major retail food groups are from BLS.

Figure 13. Dairy Price Indexes: Farm Prices Received for Dairy Products, Wholesale Fluid Milk, and Retail Fresh Milk

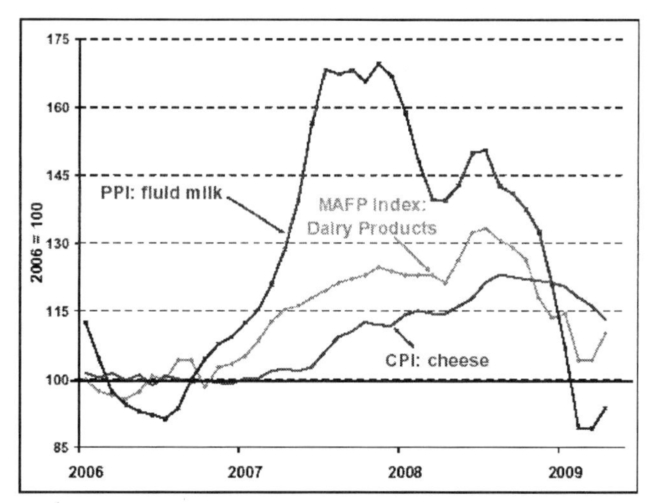


Source: Monthly average farm prices (MAFP) received are from NASS, USDA; Producer Price Index (PPI) and Consumer Price Indexes (CPI) for major retail food groups are from BLS.

Figure 14. Dairy Price Indexes: Farm Prices Received for Dairy Products, Wholesale Fluid Milk, and Retail Cheese

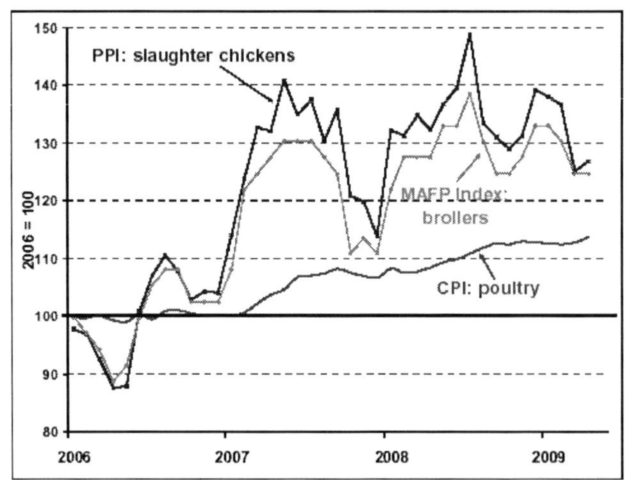


Source: Monthly average farm prices (MAFP) received are from NASS, USDA; Producer Price Index (PPI) and Consumer Price Indexes (CPI) for major retail food groups are from BLS.

Figure 15. Poultry Price Indexes: Farm Live Broilers, Wholesale Slaughter Chickens, and Retail Poultry

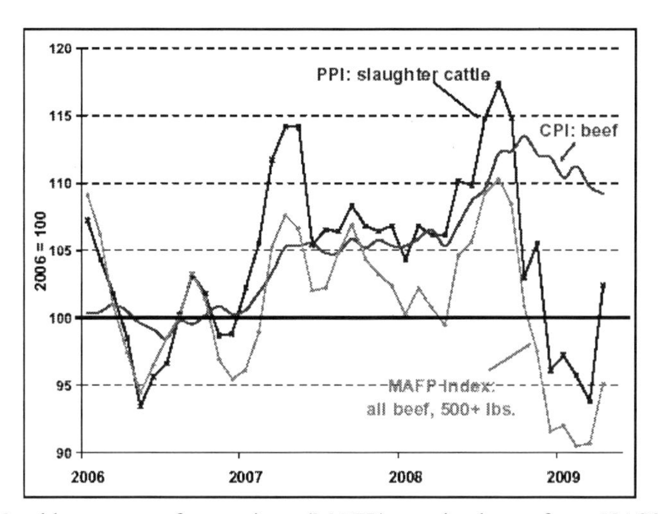


Source: Monthly average farm prices (MAFP) received are from NASS, USDA; Producer Price Index (PPI) and Consumer Price Indexes (CPI) for major retail food groups are from BLS.

Figure 16. Beef Price Indexes: Farm All-Beef (500+ lbs.), Wholesale Slaughter Cattle, and Retail Beef

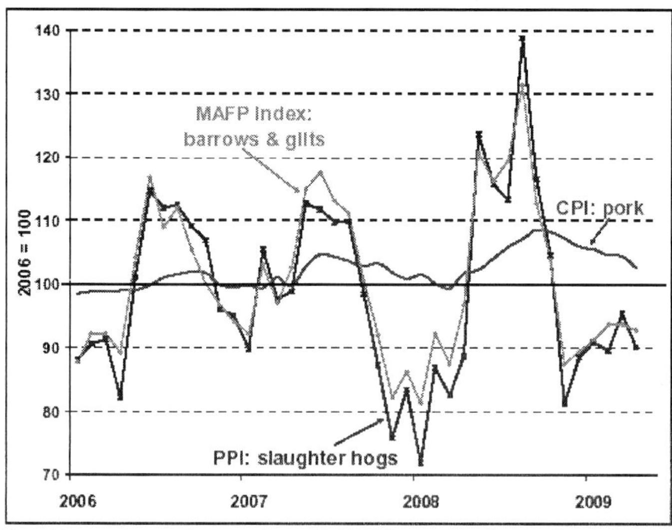


Source: Monthly average farm prices (MAFP) received are from NASS, USDA; Producer Price Index (PPI) and Consumer Price Indexes (CPI) for major retail food groups are from BLS.

Figure 17. Pork Price Indexes: Farm All-Hogs, Wholesale Slaughter Hogs, and Retail Pork

# APPENDIX A. FARM VERSUS RETAIL PRICE COMPARISONS FOR SELECT FOOD PRODUCTS

This appendix includes several figures that graph retail and farm prices for those food products that have clearly identifiable farm commodities as their raw ingredient. The farm prices are national average farm prices received as reported monthly by the National Agricultural Statistics Service (NASS) of USDA. The retail prices are U.S. city average retail prices as reported monthly by the Bureau of Labor Statistics (BLS).

Readers should note that the farm and retail prices in the following charts each relate to a different axis with different measurement scales. As a result, these charts are not useful for evaluating farm-to-retail margins. Instead they are useful for evaluating differences in direction and response behavior between farm and retail prices.

In all the figures presented here, retail prices are highly correlated with the farm price of their corresponding raw commodity. In most cases, retail prices alter their direction in response to farm prices changes with only a slight lag.

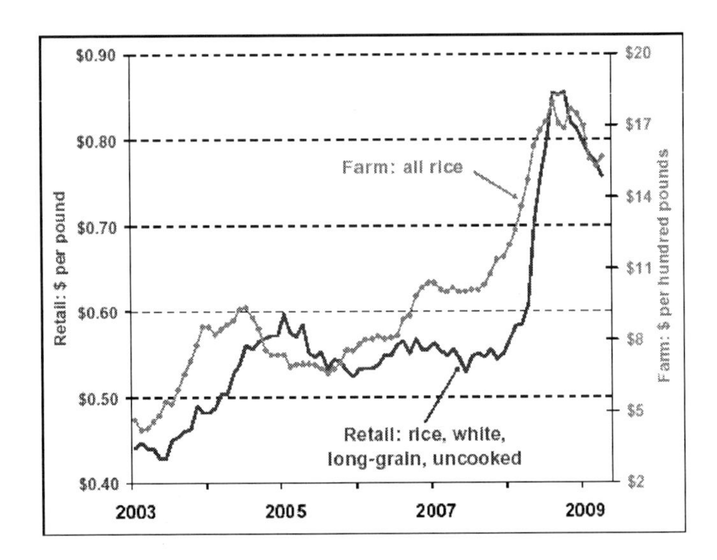


Source: Farm prices received data are from NASS, USDA; U.S. city average retail price data are from BLS.

Figure A-1. Rice Prices: Farm Rough, All-Rice versus Retail White Uncooked Long-Grain

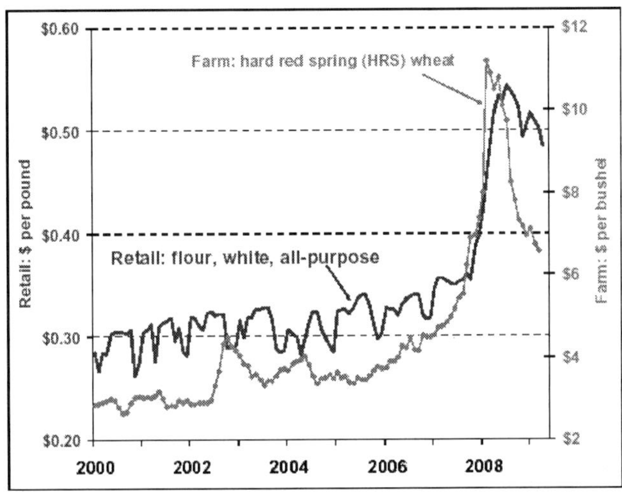


Source: Farm prices received data are from NASS, USDA; U.S. city average retail price data are from BLS.

Figure A-2. Wheat Prices: Farm High-Protein Wheat versus White All-Purpose Flour

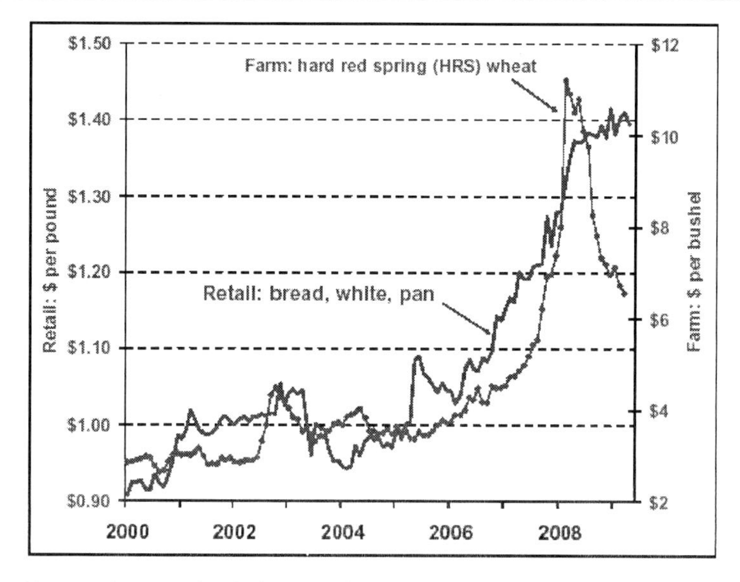


Source: Farm prices received data are from NASS, USDA; U.S. city average retail price data are from BLS.

Figure A-3. Wheat Prices: Farm High-Protein Wheat versus White Bread

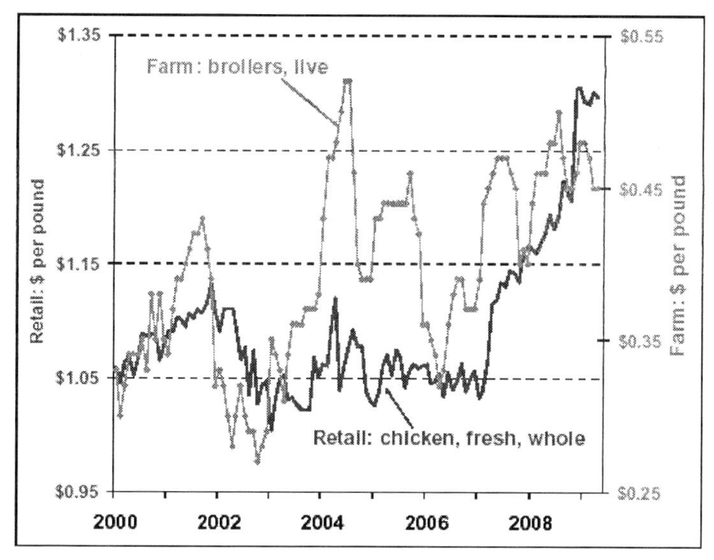


Source: Farm prices received data are from NASS, USDA; U.S. city average retail price data are from BLS.

Figure A-4. Chicken Prices: Farm Live Broilers versus Retail Fresh Whole Chicken

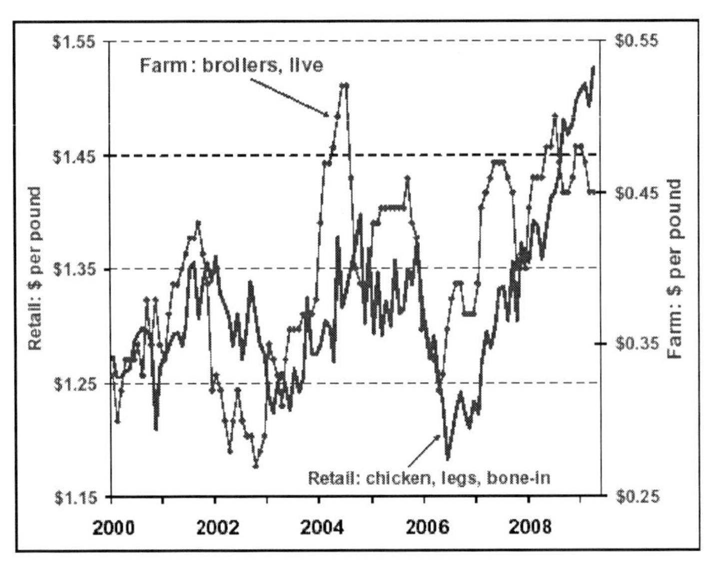


Source: Farm prices received data are from NASS, USDA; U.S. city average retail price data are from BLS.

Figure A-5. Chicken Prices: Farm Live Broilers versus Bone-in, Chicken Legs

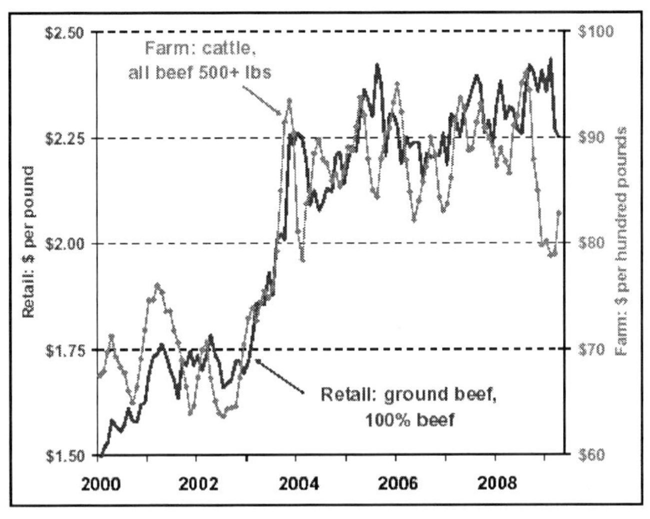


Source: Farm prices received data are from NASS, USDA; U.S. city average retail price data are from BLS.

Figure A-6. Beef Prices: Farm All-Beef Cattle (500+ lbs.) versus Retail 100% Ground Beef

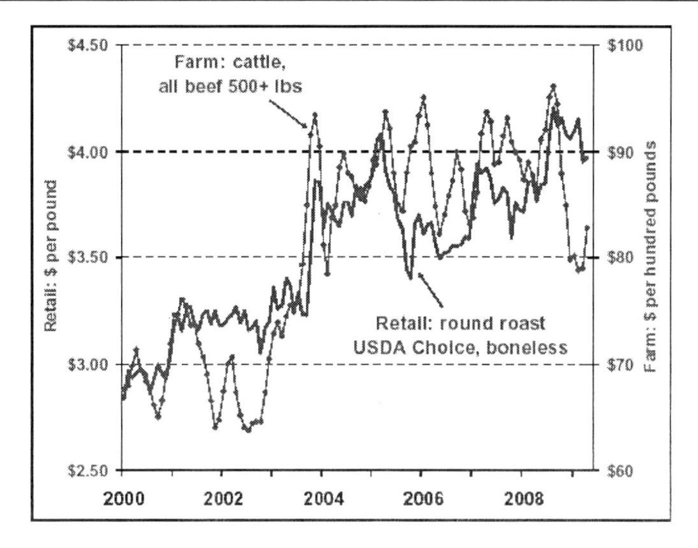


Source: Farm prices received data are from NASS, USDA; U.S. city average retail price data are from BLS.

Figure A-7. Beef Prices: Farm All-Beef Cattle (5 00+ lbs.) versus USDA Choice, Boneless Round Roast

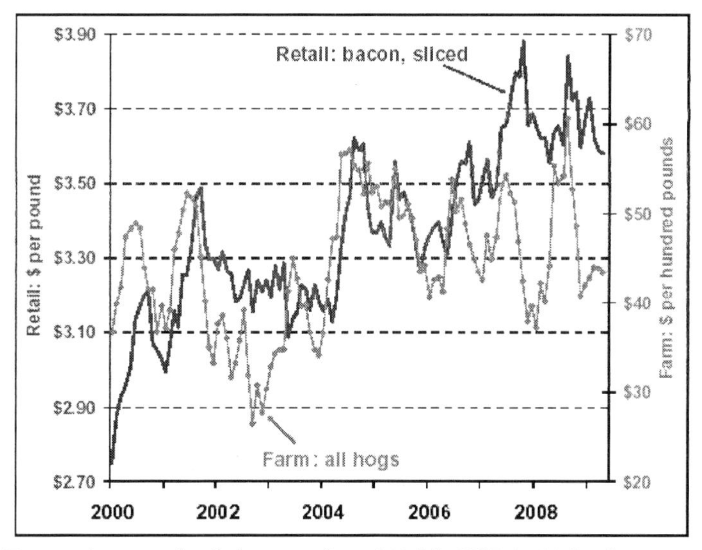


Source: Farm prices received data are from NASS, USDA; U.S. city average retail price data are from BLS.

Figure A-8. Pork Prices: Farm All-Hog versus Retail Sliced Bacon

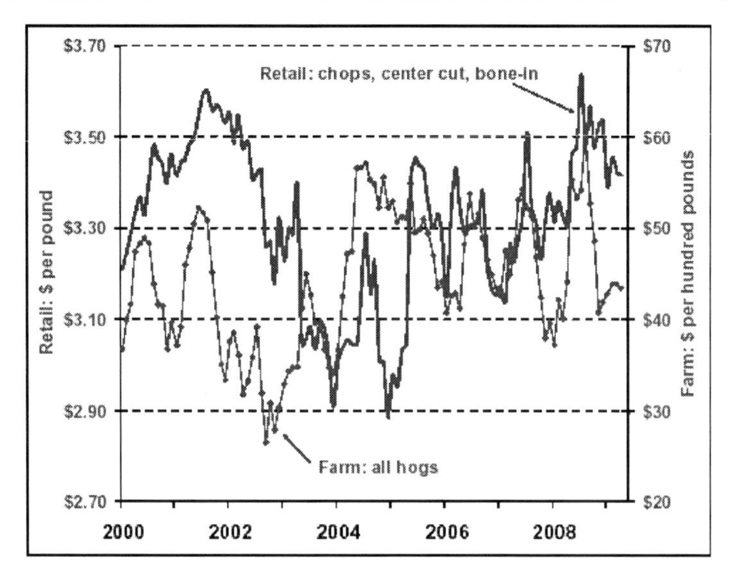


Source: Farm prices received data are from NASS, USDA; U.S. city average retail price data are from BLS.

Figure A-9. Pork Prices: Farm All-Hog versus Chops (Center-Cut, Bone-In)

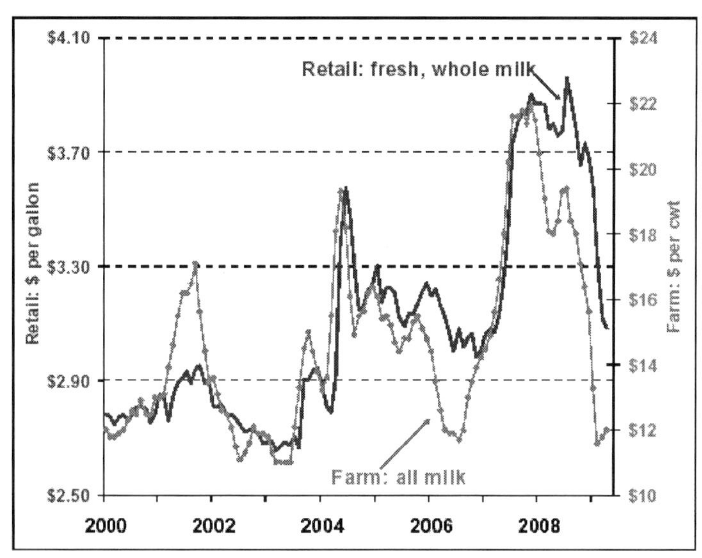


Source: Farm prices received data are from NASS, USDA; U.S. city average retail price data are from BLS.

Figure A-10. Dairy Prices: Farm All-Milk versus Retail Fresh, Whole Milk

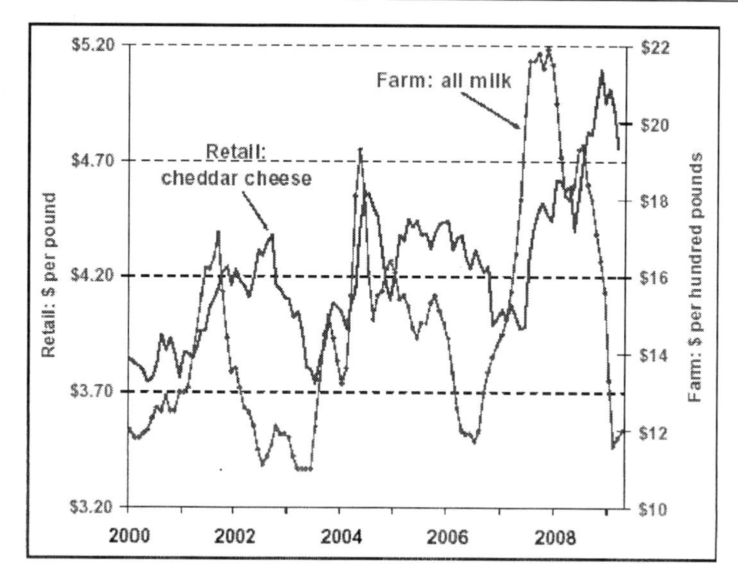


Source: Farm prices received data are from NASS, USDA; U.S. city average retail price data are from BLS.

Figure A-11. Dairy Prices: Farm All-Milk versus Retail Cheddar Cheese

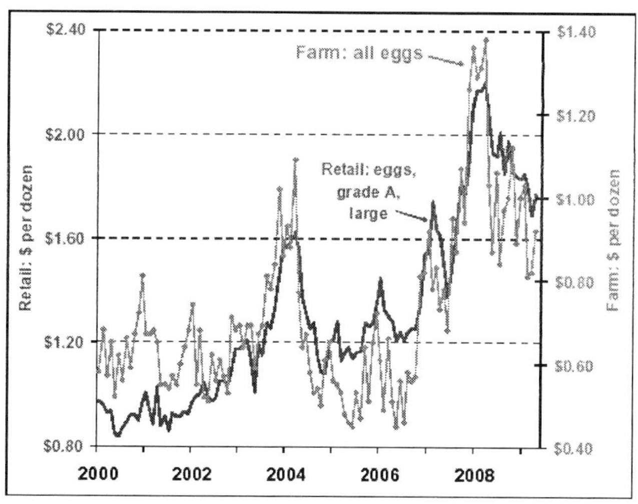


Source: Farm prices received data are from NASS, USDA; U.S. city average retail price data are from BLS.

Figure A-12. Egg Prices: Farm versus Retail

# Appendix B. Market Basket Approach to Calculating Farm-Value Share

## The Market Basket Concept Defined

For aggregate food groups, the individual food-group members are combined into market baskets derived from Bureau of Labor Statistics (BLS) data based on the Consumer Expenditure Survey (CES). This is the same data used for maintaining the Consumer Price Index (CPI).[26]

Conversion factors are used to specify the amounts of agricultural goods needed to produce a specific quantity of retail food product. For fresh fruits and vegetables, these conversion factors inflate the retail quantity by the amount necessary to compensate for waste and shrinkage that occurs as goods are prepared for sale in retail outlets. For example, ERS estimates that farmers must supply 1.031 pounds of carrots for marketers to provide 1 pound at retail.[27]

Unlike the CPI, whose market basket is updated every two years, the ERS market basket is fixed on consumer expenditures made during the 1982-1984 period. This is an inherent weakness in ERS methodology, and their own research has shown that updating the expenditure shares within the market basket to a more current period can produce significantly different results.[28]

## Constructing the Farm-Value Share

The farm value of the retail price of an individual food item (or a market basket of food items) is obtained by comparing the retail price of that food item (or basket of items) with the revenues received by farmers for the contents of a corresponding agricultural commodity (or basket of commodities).[29] In other words, this is the retail-weight equivalent of the farm products used to produce the specific retail food item, but valued at the farmgate price.[30] The retail-weight farm value must take into consideration any weight losses that might occur during the processing and marketing steps from raw to finished product, as well as the value of any by-product that results from the transformation process (an example of this is given below).

The marketing-bill component of a retail food price is the resulting difference between the retail price for that specific food item and the retail-weight-equivalent farm-value component (referred to simply as the farm value henceforth).

The calculations are fairly straightforward for individual food items that undergo only a minimal degree of transformation, such as most fresh fruits or vegetables. The calculations become more involved for food products with more processing, such as ice cream, which involves adding sugar and other ingredients to milk, or for meat products that can involve substantial by-product components such as the hide, offal, and inedible fat which are sold into secondary markets.

For aggregate groupings such as dairy products, which includes grouping milk with cheese, yogurt, ice cream, and other individual dairy products, ERS calculates a weighted-average of individual market baskets to produce a group market basket.[31] This permits the construction of farm-value shares and farm-to-retail price spreads for aggregate food groups.

## Different Methodology for Retail Cuts of Meat

ERS calculates a separate data series for estimating the farm share of retail cuts of beef, pork, and poultry. This series is not based on a market basket of retail food purchases. Instead, it is based on a combination of the cuts from a standard animal that is cut up and retailed in a standard way.[32] This concept is perhaps best understood when considering the conversion of a live steer into retail meat products. The retail value for "beef" is the weighted average price per pound of all the cuts that an animal produces less the value of by-products.[33] For example, a 1,000-pound steer produces 417 pounds of retail meat cuts, 110 pounds of edible fat, 38 pounds of variety meats, 80 pounds of hide, 40 pounds of blood, 175 pounds of inedible fats, and 140 pounds of liquids lost during processing (referred to as shrinkage).

As a steer is processed, first into wholesale carcasses or box beef, it loses weight due to the removal of bone and fat trimming, hides, hair, offal, and the like. Further bone and fat trimming is removed in converting wholesale cuts to retail cuts. The "retail-weight equivalent" of a live steer is the amount of live animal it takes to produce 1 pound of retail meat. ERS estimates that 2.4 pounds of live choice steer are needed to yield 1 pound of "standard" retail beef. Formulas also are used for determining the amount and value of by-product deductions.

Consider a hypothetical example for determining the farm-value share of retail beef. Suppose the retail price of beef is $3.40 per pound and the live weight is $0.80 per pound. Then the gross farm value is 2.4 times $0.80 = $1.92. However, an additional $0.20 per pound of by-product value must be taken into account (for each 2.4 pounds of live animal) by subtracting it from the gross farm value to give a net farm value of $1.92 - $0.20 = $1.72 per pound. Then the farm-value share is ($1.72) / ($3.40) = 50.6%. The conversion rates are held constant while the prices may vary over time, thus producing a different farm-value share.

Similarly, 1.869 pounds of 51%-to-52% lean hog produce a pound of "standard" retail pork. Consider a hypothetical pork example. Suppose the retail price of pork is $2.60 per pound and the live weight is $0.40 per pound. Then the gross farm value is 1.869 times $0.40 = $0.748. However, an additional $0.038 per pound of by-product value must be taken into account by subtracting it from the gross farm value to give a net farm value of $0.748 - $0.038 = $0.71 per pound. The resulting farm-value share is ($0.71) / ($2.60) = 27.3%.

## Author Contact Information

Randy Schnepf
Specialist in Agricultural Policy
rschnepf@crs.loc.gov, 7-4277

## Acknowledgments

This report builds upon and replaces CRS Report RS22859, *Food Price Inflation: Causes and Impacts*, by Tom Capehart and Joe Richardson; and the earlier, out-of-print CRS Report 88-761, *The Cost of Our Food*, by Geoffrey Becker.

## End Notes

[1] For more information, see CRS Report RL34474, *High Agricultural Commodity Prices: What Are the Issues?*, by Randy Schnepf.

[2] Consumer Price Index for "at-home" food purchases, as reported by the Economic Research Service, USDA, on April 22, 2009, at http://www.ers.usda.gov/Briefing/CPIFoodAndExpenditures/.

[3] For example, "Food Bill Still High? Blame 'Sticky' Prices," *Associated Press*, ©2009 Journal Gazette and Times- Courier, Oct. 19, 2008; Scott Kilman and Laren Etter, "Grain Costs

Down, Groceries Not," *Wall Street Journal*, Mar. 13, 2009; "Food Prices Continue to Rise, Despite Fall in Overall Inflation," *The Land*, online, Jan. 29, 2009.

[4] The farm-to-retail price spread expressed as a share of the retail price yields the "marketing cost" share.

[5] For more detail on the distinction between at-home and away-from-home food expenditures, see CRS Report R40545, *Consumers and Food Price Inflation*, by Randy Schnepf and Joe Richardson.

[6] The expenditure totals are reported by ERS as part of its marketing bill database. For more information, see "Calculating the Food Marketing Bill," *Amber Waves*, ERS, USDA, February 2004.

[7] The definition of total food expenditures used here is more restrictive than other food expenditure estimates produced by ERS. For example, ERS' standard measure of food expenditure (based on national account data) for 2006 is $1,032.3 billion in sales and $1,081.4 billion when including home production, institutional food, donations, and child nutrition subsidies. For more information on ERS food expenditure estimates see "Measuring the ERS Food Expenditure Series," *Food CPI, Prices and Expenditures* briefing room, ERS, USDA, at http://www.ers.usda.gov/ Briefing/CPIFoodAndExpenditures/measuringtheersfoodexpendituresseries.htm.

[8] Deflated using the general CPI for all food, Bureau of Labor Statistics (BLS).

[9] For more information, see the discussion under "Consumer Income and Expenditures," in CRS Report R40545, *Consumers and Food Price Inflation*, by Randy Schnepf and Joe Richardson.

[10] ERS uses a fixed market basket of consumer food items based on what U.S. households bought during the 1982- 1984 period for calculating farm-value shares. When a more recent (1999-2003) market basket is used, the 2004 farm- value share estimates are substantially higher at 23.5% for fresh vegetables and 26.6% for fresh fruit. For a discussion of this issue, see Hayden Stewart, *How Low Has the Farm Share of Retail Food Prices Really Fallen?* Economic Research Report No. 24, ERS, USDA, August 2006.

[11] "Calculating the Food Marketing Bill," *Amber Waves*, ERS, USDA, February 2004, available at http://www.ers.usda.gov/amberwaves/february04/indicators

[12] See "Marketing Bill: Documentation," Price Spreads from Farm to Consumer, *Food Marketing System in the U.S.* briefing room, ERS, USDA, at http://www.ers.usda.gov/Data/FarmToConsumer/componentsdoc.htm.

[13] Much of this discussion is based on William G. Tomek and Kenneth L. Robinson, "Marketing Margins," Chapter 6 of *Agricultural Product Prices*, 4th ed. (Cornell University Press, 2003), pp. 117-142.

[14] See "Price Spreads from Farm to Consumer," *Food Marketing System in the U.S.* briefing room, ERS, USDA, available at http://www.ers.usda.gov/Briefing/FoodMarketingSystem/pricespreads.htm.

[15] Ibid.

[16] For a discussion of agricultural markets for major field crops, see CRS Report RL33204, *Price Determination in Agricultural Commodity Markets: A Primer*, by Randy Schnepf.

[17] Horizontal price transmission is the linkage between prices at the same stage of the marketing chain but at different locations (also referred to as spatial price transmission). For a detailed discussion of analytical issues related to measuring and interpreting vertical price transmission, see "Analysis of Price Transmission Along the Food Chain," by Pavel Vavra and Barry Goodwin, *OECD Food, Agriculture and Fisheries Working Papers*, No. 3, OECD, Paris, 2005.

[18] Ibid., p. 3.

[19] "Marketing Margins," Chapter 6, *Agricultural Product Prices*, by William G. Tomek and Kenneth L. Robinson, 4th Edition, ©2003, Cornell University Press, p. 119.

[20] "Price Spreads from Farm to Consumer," *Food Marketing System in the U.S.* briefing room, ERS, USDA.

[21] William G. Tomek and Kenneth L. Robinson, "Marketing Margins," Chapter 6 of *Agricultural Product Prices*, 4th ed. (Cornell University Press, 2003), p. 131.

[22] Pavel Vavra and Barry Goodwin, "Analysis of Price Transmission Along the Food Chain," *OECD Food, Agriculture and Fisheries Working Papers*, No. 3, OECD, Paris, 2005, p. 3.

[23] For example, "Food Bill Still High? Blame 'Sticky' Prices," *Associated Press*, ©2009 Journal Gazette and Times- Courier, Oct. 19, 2008; Scott Kilman and Laren Etter, "Grain Costs Down, Groceries Not," *Wall Street Journal*, March 13, 2009; "Food Prices Continue to Rise, Despite Fall in Overall Inflation," *The Land*, online, Jan. 29, 2009.

[24] "U.S. Government Data Show Food Prices Falling," *CME News for Tomorrow*, © Dow Jones & Company, Inc., May 15, 2009.

[25] "Price Spreads from Farm to Consumer," *Food Marketing System in the U.S.* briefing room, ERS, USDA.

[26] For a discussion of BLS data, including the CES and CPI, see CRS Report R40545, *Consumers and Food Price Inflation*, by Randy Schnepf and Joe Richardson.

[27] For examples of conversion factors for fresh fruits and vegetables, see Tables 3-5 in Hayden Stewart, *How Low Has the Farm Share of Retail Food Prices Really Fallen?* Econ. Res. Report No. 24, ERS, USDA, Aug. 2006, pp. 10-11.

[28] For a discussion and empirical evidence, see Hayden Stewart, *How Low Has the Farm Share of Retail Food Prices Really Fallen?* Econ. Research Report No. 24, ERS, USDA, Aug. 2006.

[29] "Glossary," *Food Marketing System in the U.S.* briefing room, ERS, USDA, available at http://www.ers.usda.gov/ Briefing/FoodMarketingSystem/glossary.htm.

[30] Hayden Stewart, *How Low Has the Farm Share of Retail Food Prices Really Fallen?* Economic Research Report No. 24, ERS, USDA, August 2006.

[31] The market basket data series is available on the ERS website under "Price Spreads from Farm to Consumer: At-Home Foods by Commodity Group" at http://www.ers.usda.gov/Data/FarmToConsumer/pricespreads.htm.

[32] "Meat Price Spreads," ERS, USDA, at http://www.ers.usda.gov/Data/MeatPriceSpreads/.

[33] *Beef and Pork Values and Price Spreads Explained* by William Hahn, LDP-M-118-01, ERS, USDA, May 2004, p. 4.

In: Price Dynamics Behind Consumer Food... ISBN: 978-1-60876-892-9
Editor: Morgan D. Fitzpatrick 

*Chapter 3*

# THE IMPACT OF BIG-BOX STORES ON RETAIL FOOD PRICES AND THE CONSUMER PRICE INDEX*

***Ephraim Leibtag***
United States Department of Agriculture

## ABSTRACT

Over the past 10 years, the growth of nontraditional retail food outlets has transformed the food market landscape, increasing the variety of shopping and food options available to consumers, as well as price variation in retail food markets. This report focuses on these dynamics and how they affect food price variation across store format types. The differences in prices across store formats are especially noteworthy when compared with standard measures of food price inflation over time. Over the past 20 years, annual food price changes, as measured by the Consumer Price Index (CPI), have averaged just 3 percent per year, while food prices for similar products can vary by more than 10 percent across store formats at any one point in time. Since the current CPI for food does not fully take into account the lower price option of nontraditional retailers, a gap exists between price change as measured using scanner

* This is an edited, reformatted and augmented version of a U. S. Department of Agriculture publication dated December 2006.

data versus the CPI estimate, even for the relatively low food inflation period of 1998-2003.

**Keywords:** food prices, retail markets, CPI, dairy, nontraditional retailers

## ACKNOWLEDGMENTS

The author would like to thank Barry Krissoff, Elise Golan, and Abebayehu Tegene, as well as session participants at the 2006 AAEA meetings for their comments and suggestions.

## SUMMARY

Nontraditional retailers such as Wal-Mart, Costco, and Target have gained more of the consumer food dollar over the past 10 years. The share of sales going to traditional retailers (conventional supermarkets, superstores, and food-drug combination stores) fell from 82 percent in 1998 to 69 percent in 2003.

### What Is the Issue?

Over the past 20 years, annual food price changes, as measured by the Consumer Price Index (CPI), have averaged 3 percent per year. Meanwhile, food prices for the same item can vary by more than 10 percent from one type of store to another in a given year. The CPI measure of food price inflation is based on a sample of food items selected from a sample of retail food outlets, and the selection of stores has not been updated quickly enough to reflect the volume of food now sold through big-box stores. Since the current CPI for food does not fully account for the lower prices offered by these nontraditional retailers, including prices from all store formats would likely indicate a lower rate of price inflation than the CPI estimate.

## What Did the Study Find?

Previous studies have demonstrated that food prices at nontraditional retailers are 8-27 percent lower than at large supermarket chains. However, these comparisons across store formats did not account for quality or package-size differences for some food products. To address these concerns, comparisons in this report are for similar package sizes and more specifically defined food items: namely, dairy products and eggs.

Even when controlling for similar-sized packages, dairy prices are 5 to 25 percent lower at nontraditional retailers than at traditional supermarkets. For example, skim and low-fat milk prices are consistently 5-12 percent lower at nontraditional stores. Even more price variation exists in random-weight cheese products; a pound of Swiss cheese averaged $4.71 at grocery stores in 2003, but just $3.77 at nontraditional retailers and mass merchandisers.

Since food-at-home inflation averaged 2.2 percent per year over 1998-2003, a discrepancy of 5-25 percent in price between store formats is relatively large. If the difference in food prices across store formats applies to many food categories, the official estimates of price changes might be overstating the actual rate of change. If that is the case, another way to estimate price change might be to track consumer purchase behavior and adjust observed price changes in a given category. This could be accomplished using an expenditure-weighted measure of price change, with frequently updated measures from scanner data sources.

## How Was the Study Conducted?

This study uses ACNielsen Fresh Foods Homescan scanner panel data for 1998-2003. The annual data are from a consumer panel consisting of about 8,000 representative households across the United States; the data included purchase as well as demographic information. Panelists recorded both their UPC-coded transactions and their random-weight (non-Universal Product Code (UPC)) food purchases over the year(s) that they participate in the survey.

Average prices were calculated for a wide variety of dairy products (24 fixed-weight and 8 random-weight) commonly purchased at both traditional and nontraditional stores. The average prices were calculated by taking the total weighted expenditures for a given product and dividing by the total weighted quantity that was purchased. These average prices were then weighted using the projection factors for each household in the sample to arrive at a national average in each food category. The average prices were then used to calculate an average annual price change for each food category to compare with price change in the corresponding CPI categories.

## INTRODUCTION

One of the biggest changes in the retail food market landscape over the past 10 years has been the growth of nontraditional food outlets. Firms such as Wal-Mart, Costco, and Target—big-box stores—sell both food and nonfood products in several store formats. The supercenter, a combined mass merchandiser/full-line grocery store, is having the largest impact nationally. These stores, often over 150,000 square feet, enable the consumer to buy grocery and food staples along with clothing, electronics, and other household goods.

The supercenter, however, is not the only nontraditional format with exceptional growth over the past few years. Dollar stores, which usually sell a limited assortment of discounted products, have also expanded their food offerings with some even introducing refrigerated and frozen sections to their stores. Warehouse club stores and drugstores have also increased their food offerings and taken market share from traditional supermarkets.

These nontraditional retailers have helped to increase the variety of shopping and food options available to consumers, and variation in retail food prices has widened. Food prices can differ for a variety of reasons based on where you live, your demographic characteristics, and where you shop. Differences in labor costs, operating costs, and wholesale cost of goods sold affect the prices that retailers charge as does the competitive environment in which they operate. Competition for the U.S. consumer food dollar has intensified, and traditional retailers have been forced to lower prices, increase the number of services they provide, or improve the quality of their offerings.

Food items purchased by the average consumer span a wide range of raw and processed products. Although many features of retail food prices hold across all food categories, focusing on a specific subcategory enables one to incorporate industrywide phenomenon and commodity-specific changes into the same analysis. This report uses ACNielsen Fresh Foods Homescan scanner panel data for 1998-2003 to examine variation in dairy prices across retail store formats. Changes in the price of dairy products such as milk or cheese are often a concern for both producers and consumers.

## PREVIOUS WORK ON FOOD PRICE VARIATION

The possible differences in food prices across geographic locations and/or consumer demographics have long been investigated. Findings have been mixed, but much of the available evidence indicates that shopping opportunities for the poor are more limited than for higher income consumers and that prices are slightly higher in stores whose patrons are chiefly low- income consumers.

A review of 14 store surveys conducted between 1966 and 1996 (Kaufman et al, 1997) indicates that food prices are generally higher in smaller grocery stores than in larger supermarkets and also higher in inner-city and rural locations than in suburban locations. Costs are generally higher in these stores and locations, and it follows that prices are often higher as well.

After controlling for store type and location, however, there is little evidence of a significant relationship between neighborhood income and food prices.

But previous studies fail to account for store format as a determinant of average prices paid, and this factor has grown in significance over the past 10 years as consumers buy more of their food at nontraditional food stores. Despite significant consolidation in recent years in the supermarket industry, nontraditional retailers continue to grow much faster than supermarket chains. Various studies have demonstrated that food items at nontraditional retailers are 8-27 percent lower in price than at large supermarket chains, even after loyalty card and other special discounts are taken into account.[1]

The Bureau of Labor Statistics (BLS) currently calculates the Consumer Price Index (CPI) for food without fully accounting for the expansion of nontraditional food stores.[2] The BLS employs a linking procedure that assumes quality-adjusted prices at nontraditional retailers are exactly equal to prices at conventional supermarkets. Thus, when a supercenter or other nontraditional store replaces a conventional supermarket in the sample, BLS links the lower nontraditional price to the higher supermarket price to remove any difference. Even though packaged food items are physically identical at the two stores, the BLS procedure does not recognize any price difference between the stores. Of course, this assumption is inconsistent with actual market outcomes in which nontraditional retailers have expanded very quickly in new markets by offering substantially lower prices for a wide variety of food products. Thus, the market impacts of nontraditional retailers are understated in the CPI for food. Since the CPI for food is used as a basis for inflation in a variety of government and industry measures, this oversight has implications for estimated cost-of-living adjustments.

Hausman and Leibtag (2004), for example, compare average prices for 20 food products over a 4-year period and find that nontraditional retailers charge 27 percent lower prices, on average. This implies an upward bias of 0.32 to 0.42 percentage points in the CPI for food at home. Given that average food price inflation was 2 to 3 percent per year, this upward bias in the estimated inflation rate amounts to about 15 percent per year.

One concern with this finding is that comparisons across store formats do not account for quality or package size differences for some food products. For example, the quality of ground beef sold may differ across outlets or the package sizes available at a nontraditional outlet may be much larger than at a traditional store. To address these concerns, food product comparisons in this report are for similar package sizes and more specifically defined food products.

## DATA

This study uses ACNielsen Fresh Foods Homescan scanner panel data for 1998-2003. The data consist of about 8,000 representative U.S. households per year and include purchase and demographic information for each household in the sample. Participating panelists record both their UPC-coded transactions and their random-weight[3] (non-UPC coded) food purchases over the year(s) that they participate in the panel. This sample was used to measure the entire market basket of household purchases of food for at-home consumption.[4]

Homescan households are recruited based on their demographic information to ensure sufficient representation for demographic variables such as household income, family composition, education, and household location. Each household is equipped with an electronic home-scanning unit, and household members record every food purchase they make by scanning in the appropriate codes of the food products that they purchase for home consumption. The panel is recruited on a permanent basis, subject to turnover from normal attrition or adjustments to demographic targets necessitated by census revisions.[5] The panel is geographically dispersed and is demographically balanced to match the U.S. population as closely as possible. Homescan data are unique in that panelists record food purchases across all outlet channels, including grocery, drug, mass-merchandise, club, supercenter, and convenience stores.

Since Homescan data include no information on food bought away from home (primarily restaurant meals), one needs to assume that such purchases do not bias the average prices paid by a household for its food-at-home purchases. Once this assumption is made, Homescan data can be used for analysis of the impact of store choice on average prices paid for food-athome items. Average price paid can be aggregated across households and/or across time to measure price change for different product categories.

Standard demographic information is collected annually from each household and each household's home market/city and census region is identified for stratification purposes. Each household is then assigned a projection factor (weight) based on its demographics[6] in order to aggregate the data to be representative at the market, regional, and national level.

The information captured on a transaction level includes date of purchase, store name and channel type identifier,[7] store department identifier,[8] item description, brand name, number of units purchased, price paid, and promotions/sales/coupons used (if any). For retail stores tracked by ACNielsen in its store-level scanner data,[9] prices are taken from the store-level data to improve price accuracy.

Warehouse shipment data are used to supplement scanner-generated data collected from households or via store-level scanning, and indicate the balance of sales moving through other food retailers. This information is from census data (nonprojected, actual shipment data) supplied to ACNielsen by wholesale co-operators.

Some question the quality of household panel data when they try to reconcile it with store-level scanner data. There is a perception that the volumetric data from each source should be the same. However, panel data and store data are not always equal because measurement methodologies differ. Store-level data record millions of shopping transactions while panel data record a specific group of shoppers. In addition, panel data represent household-based purchases only, forgoing small business or institutional purchases. Panel data were used in this report in order to capture the store choice made by households. This variable would not be captured in store-level data that does not include some of the major nontraditional retailers.

## CONSUMERS SHIFT TO NONTRADITIONAL RETAILERS

Since the Homescan data track consumer food purchases across all stores, expenditure shares can be calculated for seven broad retail store formats for 1998-2003. The traditional retail group consists of conventional supermarkets, superstores, food-drug combination stores, and convenience stores. The share of sales going to this group fell from 82.3 percent in 1998 to 69.2 percent in 2003. Nontraditional outlets—including supercenters, warehouse club stores, mass merchandisers, and dollar stores—increased their share of consumer expenditures from 17.7 percent to 30.8 percent.

Within the nontraditional retail group, supercenters (primarily Wal-Mart) posted the largest increase in share from just over 3 percent in 1998 to nearly 11 percent in 2003. Warehouse club stores and dollar stores also saw significant increases in their share of the consumer food dollar as time-crunched and deal-seeking U.S. consumers look to find the best combination of prices and services at their retailer of choice.

These expenditure patterns vary by region with nontraditional retailers carving out larger shares in the Central and South regions (table 1). For example, in 2003, Wal-Mart became the top food retailer in the Dallas, Texas, market rising from sixth, in terms of market share, in less than 6 years. These shifts in the retail food market can have a large impact on the variety of foods available and average prices paid for food. And in an industry in which market leaders are usually long-time participants in a market, a dramatic change over a short period of time affects both consumers and retail food workers.

How do these changing shopping patterns impact the prices paid by consumers? Hausman and Leibtag (2004) calculated average price ratios across different types of outlets for 20 food categories and compared the prices for the food categories in traditional supermarkets versus nontraditional stores (table 2). The largest difference in average price was for lettuce. Nontraditional store prices were about 50 percent lower than traditional supermarkets over the 48-month study period. The narrowest price difference was for bottled water (5 percent less expensive in nontraditional stores). Soda was the only item with a lower price in traditional supermarkets than in nontraditional stores. Across all of the food categories, nontraditional store prices were 27 percent lower than traditional supermarkets.

These results do not account for the different mix of products that might be sold in nontraditional stores versus supermarkets; for example, types of apples could differ across stores. This quality and variety difference is difficult to quantify in consumer panel data. This report, which concentrates on dairy products, makes more restrictive comparisons in the varieties and types of products compared.

## FOOD PRICES DIFFER BETWEEN AND WITHIN MARKETS

To better understand the price differences across different store formats, average prices are calculated for a wide variety of dairy products that are commonly purchased at both traditional and nontraditional stores. Annual (1998-2003) average price estimates are calculated for 24 fixed-weight dairy products and 8 random-weight products. Average prices (tables 3, 4) are calculated by taking the total weighted expenditures for a given product and dividing by the total weighted quantity (in ounces) purchased. These average prices are then weighted using the projection factors for each household in the sample to arrive at the national average.

**Table 1. Consumer Food Expenditures at Traditional Versus Nontraditional Retailers, 1998-2003**

| Expenditure share | 1998 | 1999 | 2000 | 2001 | 2002 | 2003 |
|---|---|---|---|---|---|---|
| | *Percent* | | | | | |
| **East** | | | | | | |
| Traditional | 84 | 83 | 82 | 80 | 79 | 80 |
| Nontraditional | 16 | 17 | 18 | 20 | 21 | 20 |
| **Central** | | | | | | |
| Traditional | 84 | 82 | 80 | 78 | 74 | 74 |
| Nontraditional | 16 | 18 | 20 | 22 | 26 | 26 |
| **South** | | | | | | |
| Traditional | 80 | 77 | 73 | 70 | 66 | 65 |
| Nontraditional | 20 | 23 | 27 | 30 | 34 | 35 |
| **West** | | | | | | |
| Traditional | 81 | 80 | 77 | 76 | 72 | 72 |
| Nontraditional | 19 | 20 | 23 | 24 | 28 | 28 |

Source: ERS calculations using ACNielsen Homescan data.

**Table 2. Ratio of Supermarket and Other Outlet Prices to Nontraditional Store Prices**

| Product | Supermarkets/ Traditional retailers | All other/ Nontraditional retailers |
|---|---|---|
| Apples | 1.546 | 1.531 |
| Apple Juice | 1.585 | 1.596 |
| Bananas | 1.384 | 1.368 |
| Bread | 1.108 | 1.098 |
| Butter/Margarine | 1.096 | 1.096 |
| Cereal | 1.172 | 1.166 |
| Chicken Breast | 1.408 | 1.411 |
| Coffee | 1.373 | 1.383 |
| Cookies | 1.223 | 1.214 |
| Eggs | 1.312 | 1.305 |
| Ground Beef | 1.372 | 1.367 |
| Ham | 1.967 | 1.984 |
| Ice Cream | 1.320 | 1.331 |
| Lettuce | 2.117 | 2.107 |
| Milk | 1.207 | 1.199 |
| Potatoes | 1.412 | 1.402 |
| Soda | 0.891 | 0.974 |
| Tomatoes | 1.358 | 1.321 |
| Bottled Water | 1.058 | 1.165 |
| Yogurt | 1.413 | 1.411 |
| Average | 1.300 | 1.306 |

Source: Hausman and Leibtag (2004), calculations using ACNielsen Homescan data.

For the most part, average prices follow well-known patterns. Less processed products are subject to greater variation in price from year to year as they are more closely tied to changes in commodity prices at earlier stages of production. For example, butter and eggs vary most from year to year (12 and 8 percent), while more processed products such as ice cream vary by 2 percent per year.[10] Another interesting trend is the impact of increased sales of new products on average prices. For example, yogurt shakes and drinks, a relatively new product category with insufficient sample size to even be reported in 1998, had declining average prices for three of the four years in the sample as increased availability of the product drove its average price down 14 percent. These general price trends show the importance of defining the food categories for comparison, as trends differ across different cheese varieties, different types of milk,[11] and different package sizes. This report presents results for similar package sizes across all groups and for well-defined food products.

## NONTRADITIONAL RETAILERS DRIVE PRICE VARIATION

The growth of nontraditional retailers increases the options available to consumers and is one factor affecting price variation both within and across markets. Given that the difference in dairy prices paid is smaller across income groups (see appendix) than across regions and markets, a store's format—including physical characteristics, product offerings, business practices, and marketing strategies—is a likely determinant of variation retail food prices.

Even when controlling for similar-sized packages, dairy prices are 5-25 percent lower at nontraditional retailers than at traditional supermarkets (tables 5-8). For example, skim and low-fat milk prices are consistently 5-12 percent lower at nontraditional stores (table 5). Traditional store prices are 9.1 percent above nontraditional store prices for a representative basket of dairy products. Most dairy products are priced lower at nontraditional retailers except for Muenster cheese, butter, frozen yogurt, and sherbet categories. These products may be more heavily promoted at traditional retailers or they may not yet be sold in sufficient quantities at nontraditional retailers to have lower prices. More price variation exists in random-weight cheese products and while traditional retailers have lower prices for some products, in aggregate, nontraditional stores still have slightly lower prices even for these specialty items.

These price differences are statistically significant when modeled in an analysis of variance, and the differences between store formats are significant even after controlling for region, household income, and time.[12] For example, milk prices are analyzed using price per gallon of milk as the dependent variable in a weighted generalized regression, with store format (S), region (R), fat content of milk (M), household income (I), and a time dummy for each quarter in a given year (T).

$$P_{ijt} = F(S, R, M, I, T) \qquad i\sim\text{household}, j\sim\text{store}, t\sim\text{date} \qquad (1)$$

## Table 3. Average U.S. Dairy Prices, 1998-2003

| Product | 1998 | 1999 | 2000 | 2001 | 2002 | 2003 |
|---|---|---|---|---|---|---|
| | *Dollars* | | | | | |
| American cheese (Pound) | 2.73 | 2.87 | 2.82 | 2.83 | 2.75 | 2.67 |
| Butter (Pound) | 2.63 | 2.40 | 2.19 | 2.71 | 2.28 | 2.12 |
| Cheddar cheese (Pound) | 3.58 | 3.75 | 3.44 | 3.58 | 3.57 | 3.62 |
| Colby cheese (Pound) | 3.13 | 3.28 | 3.14 | 3.32 | 3.26 | 3.21 |
| Cottage cheese (Pound) | 1.43 | 1.50 | 1.51 | 1.54 | 1.53 | 1.50 |
| Cream cheese (Pound) | 2.46 | 2.60 | 2.51 | 2.59 | 2.54 | 2.52 |
| Extra large eggs (Dozen) | 1.10 | 1.00 | 0.99 | 1.02 | 1.03 | 1.22 |
| Farmers cheese (Pound) | 4.10 | 3.94 | 4.16 | 3.92 | 3.97 | 4.84 |
| Frozen yogurt (Half-Gallon) | 3.26 | 3.68 | 3.37 | 3.63 | 3.80 | 3.52 |
| Ice cream (Half-Gallon) | 3.07 | 3.17 | 3.18 | 3.34 | 3.31 | 3.26 |
| Jumbo eggs (Dozen) | 1.21 | 1.08 | 1.10 | 1.14 | 1.12 | 1.34 |
| Large eggs (Dozen) | 1.01 | 0.92 | 0.94 | 0.96 | 0.98 | 1.16 |
| Low-fat milk (Gallon) | 2.32 | 2.48 | 2.42 | 2.50 | 2.35 | 2.37 |
| Margarine (Pound) | 0.83 | 0.83 | 0.83 | 0.84 | 0.78 | 0.81 |
| Medium eggs (Dozen) | 0.76 | 0.69 | 0.72 | 0.77 | 0.71 | 0.93 |
| Mozzarella cheese (Pound) | 3.19 | 3.26 | 3.29 | 3.34 | 3.49 | 3.46 |
| Muenster cheese (Pound) | 3.63 | 3.83 | 3.60 | 4.03 | 4.74 | 4.82 |
| Ricotta cheese (Pound) | 1.64 | 1.70 | 1.72 | 1.76 | 1.78 | 1.76 |
| Sherbet (Half-Gallon) | 2.65 | 2.78 | 2.79 | 2.84 | 2.93 | 2.91 |
| Skim milk (Gallon) | 2.25 | 2.40 | 2.37 | 2.38 | 2.27 | 2.25 |
| Swiss cheese (Pound) | 4.28 | 4.13 | 4.22 | 4.25 | 4.48 | 4.31 |
| Whole milk (Gallon) | 2.53 | 2.67 | 2.61 | 2.72 | 2.56 | 2.60 |
| Yogurt (6 ounces) | 0.46 | 0.47 | 0.48 | 0.49 | 0.51 | 0.49 |
| Yogurt shakes (16 ounces) | NA | 2.26 | 2.20 | 2.15 | 2.18 | 1.94 |

NA = Not available.

Source: ERS calculations using ACNielsen Homescan data.

## Table 4. Average Random Weight Cheese Prices, 1998-2003

| Product | 1998 | 1999 | 2000 | 2001 | 2002 | 2003 |
|---|---|---|---|---|---|---|
| | *Dollars* | | | | | |
| American cheese (Pound) | 2.82 | 3.61 | 3.45 | 3.72 | 3.81 | 3.83 |
| Cheddar cheese (Pound) | 3.89 | 3.32 | 3.35 | 3.50 | 3.64 | 3.60 |
| Colby cheese (Pound) | 3.24 | 3.25 | 3.11 | 3.47 | 3.40 | 3.26 |
| Cream cheese (Pound) | 2.49 | 3.59 | 3.34 | 3.72 | 3.15 | 3.72 |
| Mozzarella cheese (Pound) | 3.02 | 3.27 | 3.30 | 3.67 | 3.74 | 3.87 |
| Muenster cheese (Pound) | 2.14 | 3.91 | 3.76 | 3.84 | 3.77 | 3.75 |
| Ricotta cheese (Pound) | NA | NA | 2.78 | 2.89 | 2.40 | 2.88 |
| Swiss cheese (Pound) | 4.73 | 4.55 | 4.42 | 4.63 | 4.71 | 4.70 |

NA = Not available.

Source: ERS calculations using ACNielsen Homescan data.

**Table 5. Average Milk Price Per Gallon by Store Type, 1998-2003**

| Milk type | 1998 | 1999 | 2000 | 2001 | 2002 | 2003 |
|---|---|---|---|---|---|---|
| **Skim:** | *Dollars* | | | | | |
| Grocery stores | 2.27 | 2.41 | 2.39 | 2.42 | 2.30 | 2.32 |
| Drug and convenience stores | 2.38 | 2.55 | 2.45 | 2.54 | 2.40 | 2.33 |
| Nontraditional retailers | 1.99 | 2.29 | 2.27 | 2.20 | 2.17 | 2.07 |
| **Lowfat:** | | | | | | |
| Grocery stores | 2.34 | 2.51 | 2.45 | 2.54 | 2.38 | 2.41 |
| Drug and convenience stores | 2.35 | 2.49 | 2.58 | 2.54 | 2.45 | 2.36 |
| Nontraditional retailers | 2.18 | 2.34 | 2.24 | 2.33 | 2.25 | 2.28 |
| **Whole:** | | | | | | |
| Grocery stores | 2.55 | 2.67 | 2.60 | 2.73 | 2.57 | 2.63 |
| Drug and convenience stores | 2.66 | 2.73 | 2.75 | 2.82 | 2.76 | 2.55 |
| Nontraditional retailers | 2.45 | 2.58 | 2.59 | 2.71 | 2.52 | 2.53 |

Source: ERS calculations using ACNielsen Homescan data.

**Table 6. Average Egg Prices Per Dozen by Store Type, 1998-2003**

| Egg type | 1998 | 1999 | 2000 | 2001 | 2002 | 2003 |
|---|---|---|---|---|---|---|
| **Medium:** | *Dollars* | | | | | |
| Grocery stores | 0.77 | 0.70 | 0.74 | 0.80 | 0.73 | 0.94 |
| Drug and convenience stores | 0.75 | 0.82 | 0.88 | 0.86 | 0.61 | 1.05 |
| Nontraditional retailers | 0.67 | 0.58 | 0.63 | 0.62 | 0.61 | 0.87 |
| **Large:** | | | | | | |
| Grocery stores | 1.01 | 0.93 | 0.94 | 0.97 | 0.99 | 1.18 |
| Drug and convenience stores | 1.04 | 0.94 | 0.92 | 1.05 | 1.02 | 1.02 |
| Nontraditional retailers | 0.85 | 0.72 | 0.80 | 0.82 | 0.82 | 1.07 |
| **Extra large:** | | | | | | |
| Grocery stores | 1.12 | 1.03 | 1.03 | 1.07 | 1.08 | 1.29 |
| Drug and convenience stores | 1.11 | 1.10 | 1.07 | 1.11 | 0.97 | 1.10 |
| Nontraditional retailers | 0.90 | 0.79 | 0.79 | 0.82 | 0.86 | 1.11 |
| **Jumbo:** | | | | | | |
| Grocery stores | 1.22 | 1.11 | 1.14 | 1.21 | 1.19 | 1.41 |
| Drug and convenience stores | 1.40 | 1.28 | 0.89 | 1.21 | 1.12 | 1.21 |
| Nontraditional retailers | 1.00 | 0.85 | 0.89 | 0.89 | 0.90 | 1.11 |

Source: ERS calculations using ACNielsen Homescan data.

**Table 7. Average Dairy Prices by Store Type, 1998-2003**

| Product | 1998 | 1999 | 2000 | 2001 | 2002 | 2003 |
|---|---|---|---|---|---|---|
| **American cheese (Pound):** | | | *Dollars* | | | |
| Grocery stores | 2.75 | 2.89 | 2.86 | 2.88 | 2.80 | 2.74 |
| Drug and convenience stores | 2.82 | 3.70 | 3.43 | 3.12 | 2.90 | 2.35 |
| Nontraditional retailers | 2.55 | 2.59 | 2.45 | 2.57 | 2.55 | 2.43 |
| **Butter (Pound):** | | | | | | |
| Grocery stores | 2.63 | 2.37 | 2.16 | 2.79 | 2.28 | 2.14 |
| Drug and convenience stores | 2.61 | 2.35 | 2.30 | 2.04 | 2.52 | 2.39 |
| Nontraditional retailers | 2.63 | 2.61 | 2.39 | 2.41 | 2.32 | 2.09 |
| **Cheddar cheese (Pound):** | | | | | | |
| Grocery stores | 3.59 | 3.76 | 3.52 | 3.61 | 3.60 | 3.65 |
| Drug and convenience stores | 4.46 | 5.77 | 5.57 | 4.43 | 3.85 | 4.32 |
| Nontraditional retailers | 3.45 | 3.45 | 2.76 | 3.49 | 3.40 | 3.39 |
| **Colby cheese (Pound):** | | | | | | |
| Grocery stores | 3.23 | 3.39 | 3.25 | 3.44 | 3.30 | 3.29 |
| Drug and convenience stores | 4.17 | 3.70 | 3.25 | 3.38 | 4.26 | 4.39 |
| Nontraditional retailers | 2.68 | 2.77 | 2.61 | 2.84 | 3.06 | 3.01 |
| **Cottage cheese (Pound):** | | | | | | |
| Grocery stores | 1.43 | 1.52 | 1.52 | 1.56 | 1.56 | 1.52 |
| Drug and convenience stores | 1.57 | 1.66 | 1.71 | 1.93 | 1.78 | 1.65 |
| Nontraditional retailers | 1.28 | 1.29 | 1.28 | 1.39 | 1.35 | 1.37 |
| **Cream cheese (Pound):** | | | | | | |
| Grocery stores | 2.48 | 2.64 | 2.54 | 2.64 | 2.57 | 2.58 |
| Drug and convenience stores | 2.67 | 2.45 | 2.61 | 2.17 | 2.23 | 1.88 |
| Nontraditional retailers | 2.17 | 2.14 | 2.16 | 2.30 | 2.28 | 2.26 |
| **Farmers cheese (Pound):** | | | | | | |
| Grocery stores | 4.22 | 4.38 | 4.24 | 3.96 | 4.12 | 4.83 |
| Drug and convenience stores | NA | NA | NA | NA | NA | NA |
| Nontraditional retailers | 2.97 | 2.84 | 3.20 | 3.19 | 3.17 | 5.44 |
| **Frozen yogurt (Half-Gallon):** | | | | | | |
| Grocery stores | 3.22 | 3.68 | 3.36 | 3.61 | 3.79 | 3.48 |
| Drug and convenience stores | 6.82 | 5.31 | 5.45 | 5.79 | 5.66 | 8.30 |
| Nontraditional retailers | 4.38 | 3.68 | 3.37 | 4.28 | 3.61 | 4.00 |
| **Ice cream (Half-Gallon):** | | | | | | |
| Grocery stores | 3.05 | 3.16 | 3.17 | 3.33 | 3.30 | 3.22 |
| Drug and convenience stores | 3.73 | 3.75 | 3.55 | 3.79 | 3.84 | 4.18 |

**Table 7. (Continued)**

| Product | | | | | | |
|---|---|---|---|---|---|---|
| Nontraditional retailers | **1998** | **1999** | **2000** | **2001** | **2002** | **2003** |
| **Margarine (Pound):** | 3.05 | 2.93 | 2.98 | 3.20 | 3.15 | 3.19 |
| Grocery stores | | | | | | |
| Drug and convenience stores | 0.84 | 0.84 | 0.84 | 0.86 | 0.81 | 0.84 |
| Nontraditional retailers | 0.91 | 0.89 | 0.83 | 0.75 | 0.80 | 0.68 |
| **Mozzarella cheese (Pound):** | 0.68 | 0.70 | 0.71 | 0.68 | 0.65 | 0.66 |
| Grocery stores | | | | | | |
| Drug and convenience stores | 3.21 | 3.28 | 3.32 | 3.39 | 3.55 | 3.53 |
| Nontraditional retailers | 3.43 | 3.79 | 3.89 | 3.50 | 4.07 | 2.90 |
| **Muenster cheese (Pound):** | 3.11 | 3.25 | 3.16 | 3.07 | 3.23 | 3.14 |
| Grocery stores | | | | | | |
| Drug and convenience stores | 3.57 | 3.85 | 3.58 | 4.06 | 4.75 | 4.86 |
| Nontraditional retailers | NA | NA | 2.50 | 3.58 | NA | NA |
| **Ricotta cheese (Pound):** | 4.26 | 4.61 | 4.04 | 3.78 | 4.68 | 4.71 |
| Grocery stores | | | | | | |
| Drug and convenience stores | 1.66 | 1.71 | 1.74 | 1.80 | 1.83 | 1.82 |
| Nontraditional retailers | 2.20 | 2.13 | 2.11 | 2.35 | 1.54 | 2.32 |
| **Sherbet (Half-Gallon):** | 1.32 | 1.38 | 1.59 | 1.35 | 1.43 | 1.40 |
| Grocery stores | | | | | | |
| Drug and convenience stores | 2.65 | 2.77 | 2.78 | 2.81 | 2.90 | 2.88 |
| Nontraditional retailers | 2.88 | 2.62 | 3.03 | 3.43 | 2.63 | 3.06 |
| **Swiss cheese (Pound):** | 2.43 | 2.88 | 2.82 | 3.06 | 3.19 | 3.03 |
| Grocery stores | | | | | | |
| Drug and convenience stores | 4.45 | 4.49 | 4.42 | 4.60 | 4.86 | 4.71 |
| Nontraditional retailers | 5.80 | 5.68 | 7.98 | 4.24 | 7.61 | 5.23 |
| **Yogurt (6 ounces):** | 3.63 | 3.58 | 3.90 | 3.70 | 3.82 | 3.77 |
| Grocery stores | | | | | | |
| Drug and convenience stores | 0.47 | 0.47 | 0.49 | 0.50 | 0.52 | 0.51 |
| Nontraditional retailers | 0.47 | 0.61 | 0.60 | 0.57 | 0.59 | 0.47 |
| **Yogurt shakes (16 ounces):** | 0.41 | 0.40 | 0.38 | 0.41 | 0.44 | 0.44 |
| Grocery stores | | | | | | |
| Drug and convenience stores | NA | 2.26 | 2.25 | 2.24 | 2.23 | 1.98 |
| Nontraditional retailers | NA | NA | 1.94 | 2.41 | 2.02 | 2.41 |
| | | | | | | |

Source: ERS calculations using ACNielsen Homescan data.
NA = Not available.

**Table 8. Average Prices for Random-Weight Cheeses by Store Type, 1998-2003**

| Product/retailer | 1998 | 1999 | 2000 | 2001 | 2002 | 2003 |
|---|---|---|---|---|---|---|
| | *Dollars* | | | | | |
| **American cheese (Pound):** | | | | | | |
| Grocery stores | 2.79 | 3.66 | 3.50 | 3.77 | 3.85 | 3.93 |
| Drug and convenience stores | 2.30 | 2.86 | 3.18 | 3.31 | 2.85 | 3.14 |
| Nontraditional retailers | NA | 3.29 | 3.21 | 3.30 | 2.97 | 3.19 |
| **Cheddar cheese (Pound):** | | | | | | |
| Grocery stores | 3.86 | 3.30 | 3.36 | 3.47 | 3.65 | 3.54 |
| Drug and convenience stores | 1.73 | 3.52 | 3.04 | 4.43 | 3.55 | 4.00 |
| Nontraditional retailers | NA | 3.60 | 3.34 | 3.65 | 3.55 | 3.57 |
| **Colby cheese (Pound):** | | | | | | |
| Grocery stores | 3.12 | 3.27 | 3.14 | 3.49 | 3.43 | 3.29 |
| Drug and convenience stores | 5.15 | 2.97 | 3.02 | 2.89 | 4.05 | 2.87 |
| Nontraditional retailers | NA | 3.21 | 2.76 | 3.38 | 3.03 | 3.05 |
| **Cream cheese (Pound):** | | | | | | |
| Grocery stores | 1.87 | 3.06 | 3.12 | 3.50 | 2.81 | 3.54 |
| Drug and convenience stores | 4.04 | 1.74 | 3.99 | NA | 3.49 | NA |
| Nontraditional retailers | NA | 3.38 | 1.85 | 1.65 | 2.91 | 3.41 |
| **Mozzarella cheese (Pound):** | | | | | | |
| Grocery stores | 2.93 | 3.31 | 3.41 | 3.72 | 3.85 | 3.96 |
| Drug and convenience stores | 2.85 | 4.31 | 4.09 | 2.05 | 4.02 | 4.80 |
| Nontraditional retailers | NA | 2.64 | 2.72 | 3.24 | 2.88 | 2.82 |
| **Muenster cheese (Pound):** | | | | | | |
| Grocery stores | 2.10 | 4.13 | 3.85 | 3.95 | 3.83 | 3.88 |
| Drug and convenience stores | 1.19 | 4.08 | 4.56 | 4.23 | 3.09 | 1.36 |
| Nontraditional retailers | NA | 3.41 | 3.07 | 3.42 | 3.42 | 3.19 |
| **Ricotta cheese (Pound):** | | | | | | |
| Grocery stores | NA | 1.43 | 2.39 | 3.02 | 2.43 | 2.92 |
| Drug and convenience stores | NA | NA | NA | NA | NA | NA |
| Nontraditional retailers | NA | NA | 4.57 | 6.73 | NA | 3.29 |
| **Swiss cheese (Pound):** | | | | | | |
| Grocery stores | 4.67 | 4.63 | 4.49 | 4.71 | 4.84 | 4.79 |
| Drug and convenience stores | 4.05 | 3.93 | 3.25 | 4.23 | 4.51 | 4.30 |
| Nontraditional retailers | NA | 4.30 | 3.76 | 3.98 | 3.65 | 4.23 |

NA = Not available.

Source: ERS calculations using ACNielsen Homescan data.

Average prices across formats are significantly different from one another at the 10-percent level for most items and usually at the 5-percent level or better (table 9).

Tests were run while controlling for each individual market, along with separate regressions for each market, with similar results. For example, milk prices were modeled using dummy variables for each U.S. region, household income group, milk (fat) content type, and quarter, along with the store format variables of interest. Results showed milk prices to be 6 percent lower in nontraditional retailers than in traditional stores.

**Table 9. Regression Results for Milk Prices, 1998-2003**

| Dependent variable: Price per gallon of milk | Parameter estimate | Standard error |
|---|---|---|
| **Independent variables:** | | |
| Intercept | 2.76 | 0.003 |
| **Store format:** | | |
| Grocery stores | Reference format | |
| Drug and convenience stores | 0.04 | 0.002 |
| Nontraditional retailers | -0.16 | 0.002 |
| Other | -0.20 | 0.003 |
| **Milk type:** | | |
| Skim | -0.24 | 0.002 |
| Lowfat | -0.17 | 0.001 |
| Whole | Reference type | |
| **Region:** | | |
| East | 0.12 | 0.002 |
| South | -0.08 | 0.002 |
| Central | 0.21 | 0.002 |
| West | Reference region | |
| **Household income:** | | |
| < $25,000 | -0.04 | 0.002 |
| $25,000 - $49,999 | -0.03 | 0.002 |
| $50,000 - $70,000 | -0.01 | 0.002 |
| > $70,000 | Reference income group | |
| Quarter time dummy variables | Jointly significant at the 5% level | |
| $R^2$ | 0.12 | |

Source: ERS calculations using ACNielsen Homescan data.

## DAIRY CPI ESTIMATES OVERSTATE PRICE CHANGE

Price differences across store formats are especially noteworthy when compared with standard measures of food price inflation over time. Over the past 20 years, annual food price changes, as measured by the CPI, have averaged just 3 percent per year. Differences of more than 5 percent in food prices are driven by differences in store formats, which largely account for the regional and market variation in prices observed across the United States. Since price differences are larger across store formats than over time, it is instructive to investigate the impact of cross-outlet variation on estimates of food price inflation.

The standard measure of food price inflation, as calculated in the CPI, is based on a sample of food items selected from a sample of retail food outlets. The selection of stores has not been updated as fast as the change in shopping behavior, so some of the price differences between outlet types are not accounted for in the CPI for food.

Three aggregate CPI indices can be compared with the outlet-specific price calculations in this report—dairy, eggs, and butter/margarine. The overall dairy CPI has four subgroups—milk, cheese, ice cream, and other dairy (table 10). In general, average price change as measured by scanner data show lower levels of price change than reported by BLS. This result is consistent with earlier work by MacDonald (1995) and echoes the often- cited criticism by many in the food industry that increased competition from nontraditional retail outlets dampens inflationary price increases as measured in the CPI.

In 4 of the 5 years compared in this study, dairy and egg price inflation are smaller in the scanner data than the CPI data (table 10). An exception is found in the butter and margarine category in which the scanner data shows lower rates of inflation (or greater rates of deflation) in just 2 of the 5 years. Also interesting is that the large recorded increase in butter and margarine prices in the 2001 CPI was almost completely unobserved in the scanner data, implying that consumers react quickly to sharp price increases by changing their shopping behavior to minimize the impact of large price increases. Overall, these comparisons imply that the CPI values published by BLS are 0.5 to 2.5 percentage points above scanner data estimates of annual price change. This is especially noteworthy considering that annual food-at-home price inflation averaged just 2.2 percent over 1999-2003.

For these dairy categories, then, the CPI would seem to overstate food price inflation, but the exact magnitude is more difficult to quantify given differences in these data sources. The CPI is derived from store-based price information and does not fully take into account changes in consumer shopping behavior. This may cause some price changes to be missed in the CPI calculation. On the other hand, Homescan data tracks consumer shopping behavior and picks up changes as they occur, but may understate food price inflation if consumers in the panel are more price sensitive and/or deal savvy in their shopping behavior than the average U.S. household. A hybrid approach that uses scanner data to track current shopping patterns but quality adjusts the current CPI for food by incorporating information on shopping behavior from other sources may be the best solution to this discrepancy. For a more detailed discussion of these issues, see Hausman and Leibtag (2004, 2005).

## CONCLUSION

Changes in food retailing affect food prices, as well as the variety of products and services available to consumers. With average dairy food prices 5- 25 percent lower at nontraditional retailers, the growing presence of these stores will decrease the average prices paid by consumers for these products. While different product mixes may exist at different stores, the price differences estimated in this analysis across different outlet types are unlikely to arise primarily from different product mixes since comparisons are made for similar package sizes and product characteristics. These lower prices and increased options should provide a net welfare benefit to U.S. consumers, but it remains to be seen if the overall economy will benefit from these new retail formats, particularly when taking into account the impact on traditional retailers, food retail workers, food manufacturers, and agricultural producers.

As consumers turn in greater numbers to nontraditional stores for their common grocery items, the prices and variety of products available at those stores will have an increasingly important role in retail food markets. A nontraditional store's entry into a new geographic market creates a direct price effect by offering a lower price option to consumers and an indirect price effect by causing traditional supermarkets to lower their prices because of the increased competition.

**Table 10. Average Annual Change in Prices, ACNielsen Homescan versus BLS, 1999-2003**

| | 1999 | 2000 | 2001 | 2002 | 2003 |
|---|---|---|---|---|---|
| | | | *Percent* | | |
| ACN Dairy total | 6.0 | -1.6 | 3.5 | -1.2 | -0.1 |
| BLS Dairy total | 5.8 | 0.7 | 4.0 | 0.6 | -0.1 |
| ACN Milk | 2.3 | -0.8 | 1.0 | -1.9 | 0.2 |
| BLS Milk | 6.2 | 0.2 | 4.5 | -1.9 | 0.8 |
| ACN Cheese | 3.0 | -0.8 | 1.9 | 0.3 | 0.3 |
| BLS Cheese | 6.8 | 0.1 | 2.9 | 1.4 | -0.4 |
| ACN Other dairy | 0.0 | 0.1 | 0.0 | 0.2 | -0.3 |
| BLS Other dairy | 5.2 | 2.1 | 2.8 | 1.8 | 0.4 |
| ACN Ice cream | 0.6 | -0.2 | 0.5 | 0.0 | -0.3 |
| BLS Ice cream | 4.0 | 1.7 | 5.5 | 3.3 | -2.0 |
| ACN Eggs | -0.4 | 0.1 | 0.2 | 0.0 | 1.1 |
| BLS Eggs | -5.4 | 3.0 | 3.4 | 1.3 | 13.8 |
| ACN Butter and margarine | -0.3 | -0.3 | 1.0 | -0.7 | -0.2 |
| BLS Butter and margarine | -0.1 | -3.1 | 14.9 | -2.6 | -1.2 |

ACN = ACNielsen; BLS = Bureau of Labor Statistics

Source: ERS calculations using ACNielsen Homescan data, BLS-CPI data.

The current CPI for food does not fully take into account the lower price offered by a nontraditional retailer. Currently, the BLS links out the lower prices of a nontraditional retailer by assuming that any price variation between a traditional and nontraditional retailer is a store-based difference in quality of service versus simply a lower price for similar (or even identical) products. If this assumption were correct, the gain in market share by nontraditional outlets would not be so significant and ongoing.

A more appropriate approach to price change estimation would be to track consumer purchase behavior and adjust observed price changes in a given category. This could be accomplished using an expenditure-weighted measure of price change with frequently updated measures from scanner data sources. A frequently updated expenditure-weighted price calculation could be applied to industries in which consumer purchase information is readily available, such as the grocery industry. This system could be applied elsewhere as better tracking information is developed across other sectors.

A significant difference exists between price change as measured using scanner data and the CPI estimate of price change, even for the relatively low food inflation period of 1998-2003 covered in this report. This study estimates that the CPI for dairy products overstates change in food prices by 0.5 to 2.5 percentage points per year for the dairy, eggs, and butter/margarine categories. Future research is necessary to estimate whether these differences are as pronounced in other food categories. The more common this difference is, the more important a correction to the official estimates of price change is to getting an accurate measure of food price inflation.

Traditional food retailers that have lowered prices and/or increased the quality and variety of the services they provide have remained competitive, while those that have not adapted have struggled. Retailers that do not adjust quickly lose market share and may choose to exit a market where they once were dominant; in some cases, they exit food retailing entirely. For food wholesalers, distributors, and others involved in the food supply chain, expanding and maintaining relationships with nontraditional retailers will be crucial to ensuring that their products are available to the U.S. consumer in the future.

## REFERENCES


Basker, Emek. (Sept. 2005). "Selling a Cheaper Mousetrap: Wal-Mart's Effect on Retail Prices," *Journal of Urban Economics, 58*, 2, pp. 203-229.

Betancourt, Roger, and David Gautschi. (June 1988). "The Economics of Retail Firms," *Managerial and Decision Economics, 9*, 133-144.

Cage, R. (Dec. 1996). "New Methodology for Selecting CPI Outlet Samples," *Monthly Labor Review*, p. 49.

Callahan, P., and A. Zimmerman. "Grocery Chains Fighting Wal-Mart for Market Share," *Wall Street Journal*, May 31, 2003.

Chung, Chanjin, and Samuel L. Myers, Jr. (Number 2/Winter 1999). "Do the Poor Pay More for Food? An Analysis of Grocery Store Availability and Food Price Disparities," *Journal of Consumer Affairs,* 33, 276-296.

Currie, N., H. Kim, and A. Jain. (Dec. 2003). "Price Gap Tightens, Competition Looks Hot Hot Hot," *UBS Investment Research.*

Finke, Michael S., Wen S. Chern, and Jonathan J. Fox. (Number 1/Spring 1997). "Do the Urban Poor Pay More for Food? Issues in Measurement," *Advancing the Consumer Interest,* 9, 13-17.

Food Marketing Institute.(2001). *2000-2001 Annual Financial Review.* Washington, DC.

Hausman, J. (Oct. 2003). "Sources of Bias and Solutions to Bias in the CPI," *Journal of Economic Perspectives.*

Hausman, J., and E. Leibtag. (Aug. 2004). "CPI Bias from Supercenters: Does the BLS Know that Wal-Mart Exists?" NBER Working Paper #20712, National Bureau of Economic Research, Cambridge, MA.

Hausman, J., and E. Leibtag, (Dec. 2005). "Consumer Benefits from Increased Competition in Shopping Outlets: Measuring the Effect of Wal-Mart," NBER Working Paper #11809, National Bureau of Economic Research, Cambridge, MA.

Hayes, Lashawan Richburg. (Sept. 2000). "Do the Poor Pay More? An Empirical Investigation of Price Dispersion in Food Retailing." Industrial Relations Section Working Paper 446. Princeton University, Princeton, NJ,

Kaufman, Phillip R., James M. MacDonald, Steven M. Lutz, and David M. Smallwood. (Nov. 1997). *Do the Poor Pay More for Food? Item Selection and Price Differences Affect Low-Income Household Food Costs.* U.S. Department of Agriculture, Economic Research Service. AER 759.

Leibtag, Ephraim S., and Phil R. Kaufman. (June 2003). *Exploring Food Purchase Behavior of Low-Income Households: How Do They Economize?* U.S. Department of Agriculture, Economic Research Service, AIB-747-07.

Little, P. (June 2004). "Channel Blurring Redefines the Grocery Market," *Competitive Edge.*

MacDonald, James M. (Sept.-Dec., 1995). "Consumer Price Index Overstates Food-Price Inflation," *Food Review*, Economic Research Service, USDA.

Reinsdorf, M. (1993). "The Effect of Outlet Price Differentials in the U.S. Consumer Price Index," *Price Measurements and Their Uses* (M.F. Foss et. al, eds.), Chicago. University of Chicago Press.

Schultze, C., and C. Mackie (eds.). (2002). *At What Price?* National Academy of Sciences Press, Washington, DC.

# APPENDIX: FOOD PRICE DIFFERENCES ACROSS REGIONS, MARKETS, AND INCOME LEVELS

Since the Homescan data were constructed based on a stratified random sample, with households as the primary sampling unit and the sample of households matching census-based demographic/geographic targets, one can estimate average prices by region and major market for cross-market comparison.[13] There was no known or intentional clustering in the sample construction.

## Regional Differences

A common question regarding retail food prices is the extent to which they vary across regions. Appendix tables 1 and 2 show average dairy prices across 4 regions for 24 commonly purchased dairy department products. In general, dairy prices are lowest in the Midwest and highest in the West.[14] Prices in the South are 3.5 percent below those in the East. Although the magnitude of these differences varies from product to product, regional differences in food prices are important for any policy or program that adjusts for food costs. A national average price or cost may be inappropriate measure for a particular region or market. Regional adjustments that take into account these differences would improve any benefits or welfare program attempting to account for cost-of-living differences both over time and across markets.

These differences are highlighted by looking at average milk prices per gallon across regions. Both skim and low-fat milk prices were highest in the South, while whole-milk prices were highest in the West for three of the study years and highest in the South for two of the study years. Interestingly, price variation is widest, on average, for skim milk, with the difference between highest and lowest regional price per year ranging from 15 to 30 percent (8-15 percent for low-fat and 7-17 percent for whole). The wider regional price range for skim milk may be due to differences in milk content and wholesale costs, in demand for various milk products, or pricing strategies practiced by retailers.

Price differences across regions are especially noteworthy given the relatively stable level of price inflation in each region over 1998-2003. The highest average annual inflation rate was in the East (1.78 percent), while the

West, South, and Midwest regions averaged 1.77, 1.52, and 0.84 percent, respectively.

There are a variety of possible explanations for the difference in dairy prices across regions. Regional price variation may be a function of differences in production and transportation costs, consumer preferences and/or demographics, and level of retail competition in a given market. Due to the unique nature of the ACNielsen Homescan data, one can compare average prices across major U.S. markets, store types, or household demographics to better illuminate possible causes of the observed regional price variation.

## Market Differences

Appendix tables 3 and 4 present average dairy prices in eight major U.S. markets, as well as the average price for nonmetro consumers.[15] For the most part, the major markets follow the general regional patterns. Chicago (Midwest) has the lowest average market prices, while Los Angeles and San Francisco (West) have the highest. The only exception to the regional patterns is in Philadelphia where prices were second lowest, on average, and not statistically different from average prices in Chicago and Atlanta.[16] Nonmetro consumers pay lower average prices for dairy products than do consumers in any of the eight major markets.

These statistically significant differences in prices across U.S. markets indicate differences in both food costs and consumer behavior. Price variation at the retail level may be a function of both supply and demand conditions in a given market. On the supply side, differences in transaction, marketing, or operating costs may explain some of the retail price variation. On the demand side, consumer preferences for different retail store formats will generate differences in average prices across markets.

## Household Income Differences

Consumers can affect the price they pay for foods through their purchase behavior: this can include using coupons, checking the newspaper for sale items, or traveling to a store offering lower prices. Do average prices paid differ across income groups? How do these differences compare with geographical price differences? Households in the ACNielsen data were placed into four income groups (appendix tables 5 and 6). Overall, higher income households pay higher average prices for dairy products, but some of this difference may be due to differences in purchase choices within a category. However, these differences are smaller than the regional and market differences in prices. Low-income households (income less than $25,000) pay an average of 3.4 percent less for their dairy products, and high-income households pay 6.0 percent more than middle-income households.

Since regional and market differences are larger than differences in prices paid by income groups, there must be more behind the geographical differences than just the demographic makeup of a region or market. The retail food stores available to consumers in a given market will affect average prices paid for food since stores use price differences as one way to differentiate themselves from competitors.

**Appendix Table 1. Average Dairy Prices by U.S. Region, 1998-2003**

| Product | 1998 | 1999 | 2000 | 2001 | 2002 | 2003 |
|---|---|---|---|---|---|---|
| | | | *Dollars* | | | |
| **American cheese (Pound)** | | | | | | |
| East | 2.72 | 2.84 | 2.75 | 2.89 | 2.84 | 2.83 |
| Midwest | 2.65 | 2.64 | 2.55 | 2.67 | 2.56 | 2.41 |
| South | 2.69 | 2.91 | 2.89 | 2.73 | 2.66 | 2.58 |
| West | 3.05 | 3.17 | 3.26 | 3.38 | 3.31 | 3.25 |
| **Butter (Pound)** | | | | | | |
| East | 2.64 | 2.40 | 2.20 | 2.71 | 2.24 | 2.03 |
| Midwest | 2.48 | 2.22 | 2.09 | 2.55 | 2.08 | 2.03 |
| South | 2.74 | 2.58 | 2.25 | 2.76 | 2.30 | 2.12 |
| West | 2.66 | 2.41 | 2.23 | 2.84 | 2.54 | 2.34 |
| **Cheddar cheese (Pound)** | | | | | | |
| East | 3.57 | 3.70 | 3.62 | 3.70 | 3.67 | 3.71 |
| Midwest | 3.25 | 3.47 | 3.21 | 3.28 | 3.27 | 3.34 |
| South | 3.61 | 3.83 | 3.38 | 3.59 | 3.61 | 3.61 |
| West | 4.12 | 3.96 | 3.77 | 4.01 | 3.92 | 4.01 |
| **Colby cheese (Pound)** | | | | | | |
| East | 3.34 | 3.59 | 3.40 | 3.78 | 4.02 | 3.04 |
| Midwest | 3.16 | 3.37 | 3.07 | 3.21 | 3.10 | 3.10 |
| South | 2.99 | 3.09 | 3.15 | 3.40 | 3.32 | 3.25 |
| West | 3.47 | 3.42 | 3.27 | 3.37 | 3.44 | 3.79 |

**Appendix Table 1. (Continued)**

| Product | 1998 | 1999 | 2000 | 2001 | 2002 | 2003 |
|---|---|---|---|---|---|---|
| | *Dollars* | | | | | |
| **Cottage cheese (Pound)** | | | | | | |
| East | 1.52 | 1.61 | 1.63 | 1.66 | 1.70 | 1.65 |
| Midwest | 1.29 | 1.37 | 1.36 | 1.39 | 1.38 | 1.40 |
| South | 1.44 | 1.46 | 1.49 | 1.50 | 1.50 | 1.45 |
| West | 1.60 | 1.73 | 1.75 | 1.79 | 1.72 | 1.66 |
| **Cream cheese (Pound)** | | | | | | |
| East | 2.53 | 2.62 | 2.55 | 2.66 | 2.50 | 2.56 |
| Midwest | 2.34 | 2.44 | 2.36 | 2.45 | 2.35 | 2.33 |
| South | 2.4 | 2.59 | 2.40 | 2.47 | 2.44 | 2.38 |
| West | 2.64 | 2.83 | 2.83 | 2.97 | 3.11 | 3.11 |
| **Extra large eggs (Dozen)** | | | | | | |
| East | 1.18 | 1.11 | 1.09 | 1.10 | 1.09 | 1.28 |
| Midwest | 0.97 | 0.85 | 0.86 | 0.90 | 0.89 | 1.05 |
| South | 1.04 | 0.96 | 0.93 | 0.96 | 1.00 | 1.18 |
| West | 1.32 | 1.16 | 1.20 | 1.18 | 1.20 | 1.47 |
| **Farmers cheese (Pound)** | | | | | | |
| East | 3.41 | 3.52 | 4.21 | 4.05 | 3.87 | 4.24 |
| Midwest | 4.24 | 3.10 | 3.40 | 3.22 | 2.79 | 3.85 |
| South | 3.76 | 5.37 | 5.56 | 4.42 | 4.41 | 4.43 |
| West | 5.76 | 5.14 | 4.35 | 3.18 | 5.87 | 6.67 |
| **Frozen yogurt (Half-Gallon)** | | | | | | |
| East | 3.09 | 4.36 | 3.02 | 3.52 | 4.55 | 3.83 |
| Midwest | 3.54 | 3.33 | 3.50 | 3.89 | 3.52 | 3.08 |
| South | 2.96 | 3.05 | 3.30 | 3.33 | 3.08 | 3.18 |
| West | 4.44 | 4.07 | 4.30 | 4.67 | 5.21 | 4.80 |
| **Ice cream (Half-Gallon)** | | | | | | |
| East | 2.88 | 3.13 | 3.02 | 3.22 | 3.28 | 3.25 |
| Midwest | 2.85 | 2.99 | 3.07 | 3.19 | 3.01 | 2.88 |
| South | 3.09 | 3.19 | 3.2 | 3.37 | 3.33 | 3.32 |
| West | 3.42 | 3.37 | 3.43 | 3.60 | 3.61 | 3.62 |
| **Jumbo eggs (Dozen)** | | | | | | |
| East | 1.35 | 1.32 | 1.22 | 1.31 | 1.30 | 1.51 |
| Midwest | 1.10 | 1.00 | 1.02 | 1.09 | 1.02 | 1.21 |
| South | 1.14 | 0.95 | 1.03 | 1.05 | 1.07 | 1.26 |

**Appendix Table 1. (Continued)**

| Product | 1998 | 1999 | 2000 | 2001 | 2002 | 2003 |
|---|---|---|---|---|---|---|
| | *Dollars* | | | | | |
| West | 1.28 | 1.23 | 1.20 | 1.25 | 1.21 | 1.49 |
| **Large eggs (Dozen)** | | | | | | |
| East | 1.11 | 1.04 | 1.04 | 1.05 | 1.06 | 1.28 |
| Midwest | 0.87 | 0.77 | 0.80 | 0.82 | 0.84 | 1.02 |
| South | 0.96 | 0.87 | 0.89 | 0.92 | 0.92 | 1.11 |
| West | 1.17 | 1.09 | 1.13 | 1.19 | 1.25 | 1.40 |
| **Low-fat milk (Gallon)** | | | | | | |
| East | 2.34 | 2.52 | 2.45 | 2.61 | 2.47 | 2.50 |
| Midwest | 2.18 | 2.39 | 2.32 | 2.34 | 2.22 | 2.22 |
| South | 2.48 | 2.57 | 2.54 | 2.63 | 2.54 | 2.55 |
| West | 2.30 | 2.47 | 2.34 | 2.47 | 2.22 | 2.26 |
| **Margarine (Pound)** | | | | | | |
| East | 0.94 | 0.91 | 0.94 | 0.92 | 0.91 | 0.92 |
| Midwest | 0.80 | 0.78 | 0.79 | 0.81 | 0.76 | 0.76 |
| South | 0.78 | 0.79 | 0.77 | 0.76 | 0.71 | 0.73 |
| West | 0.86 | 0.89 | 0.89 | 0.93 | 0.88 | 0.95 |
| **Medium eggs (Dozen)** | | | | | | |
| East | 0.86 | 0.78 | 0.83 | 0.90 | 0.85 | 1.01 |
| Midwest | 0.67 | 0.58 | 0.66 | 0.68 | 0.60 | 0.82 |
| South | 0.72 | 0.68 | 0.68 | 0.73 | 0.70 | 0.89 |
| West | 1.02 | 0.84 | 0.89 | 0.90 | 0.79 | 1.08 |
| **Mozzarella cheese (Pound)** | | | | | | |
| East | 2.84 | 2.89 | 2.91 | 3.01 | 3.07 | 3.09 |
| Midwest | 3.09 | 3.27 | 3.12 | 3.14 | 3.50 | 3.48 |
| South | 3.19 | 3.30 | 3.25 | 3.41 | 3.42 | 3.42 |
| West | 3.73 | 3.84 | 3.90 | 3.89 | 4.18 | 4.13 |
| **Muenster cheese (Pound)** | | | | | | |
| East | 3.74 | 4.01 | 3.94 | 4.26 | 4.49 | 4.26 |
| Midwest | 3.29 | 3.88 | 3.34 | 3.41 | 4.17 | 4.04 |
| South | 3.53 | 3.55 | 3.23 | 4.00 | 4.78 | 5.37 |
| West | 4.66 | 4.61 | 5.49 | 5.00 | 5.73 | 5.31 |
| **Ricotta cheese (Pound)** | | | | | | |
| East | 1.47 | 1.57 | 1.53 | 1.59 | 1.65 | 1.64 |
| Midwest | 1.94 | 2.07 | 2.01 | 2.03 | 1.99 | 2.02 |

**Appendix Table 1. (Continued)**

| Product | 1998 | 1999 | 2000 | 2001 | 2002 | 2003 |
|---|---|---|---|---|---|---|
| | *Dollars* | | | | | |
| South | 1.67 | 1.64 | 1.74 | 1.74 | 1.70 | 1.7 |
| West | 2.16 | 2.17 | 2.27 | 2.33 | 2.33 | 2.3 |
| **Sherbet (Half-Gallon)** | | | | | | |
| East | 2.74 | 3.02 | 3.07 | 2.92 | 3.03 | 3.21 |
| Midwest | 2.50 | 2.41 | 2.50 | 2.48 | 2.62 | 2.63 |
| South | 2.75 | 2.84 | 2.96 | 3.03 | 3.10 | 3.02 |
| West | 2.63 | 2.83 | 2.67 | 3.05 | 2.94 | 2.86 |
| **Skim milk (Gallon)** | | | | | | |
| East | 2.29 | 2.47 | 2.38 | 2.50 | 2.44 | 2.46 |
| Midwest | 2.11 | 2.30 | 2.28 | 2.27 | 2.15 | 2.14 |
| South | 2.43 | 2.57 | 2.58 | 2.60 | 2.53 | 2.55 |
| West | 2.16 | 2.23 | 2.21 | 2.29 | 2.10 | 1.95 |
| **Swiss cheese (Pound)** | | | | | | |
| East | 4.07 | 4.30 | 4.36 | 4.35 | 4.54 | 4.63 |
| Midwest | 4.19 | 4.21 | 4.48 | 4.16 | 4.31 | 4.12 |
| South | 4.38 | 4.02 | 4.23 | 4.31 | 4.53 | 4.40 |
| West | 4.30 | 4.26 | 3.97 | 4.13 | 4.49 | 4.14 |
| **Whole milk (Gallon)** | | | | | | |
| East | 2.55 | 2.73 | 2.67 | 2.76 | 2.59 | 2.72 |
| Midwest | 2.38 | 2.53 | 2.49 | 2.57 | 2.43 | 2.34 |
| South | 2.56 | 2.66 | 2.65 | 2.73 | 2.68 | 2.74 |
| West | 2.59 | 2.75 | 2.55 | 2.81 | 2.38 | 2.45 |
| **Yogurt (6 ounces)** | | | | | | |
| East | 0.48 | 0.49 | 0.50 | 0.51 | 0.54 | 0.52 |
| Midwest | 0.46 | 0.48 | 0.49 | 0.51 | 0.51 | 0.49 |
| South | 0.45 | 0.44 | 0.45 | 0.45 | 0.48 | 0.46 |
| West | 0.46 | 0.45 | 0.48 | 0.49 | 0.52 | 0.50 |
| **Yogurt shakes (16 ounces)** | | | | | | |
| East | NA | NA | 2.22 | 2.37 | 2.34 | 1.84 |
| Midwest | NA | 2.25 | 2.14 | 2.18 | 2.17 | 1.87 |
| South | NA | 2.26 | 2.19 | 2.15 | 2.09 | 1.90 |
| West | NA | NA | 2.27 | 2.02 | 2.18 | 2.15 |

Source: ERS calculations using ACNielsen Homescan data.

NA = Not available.

**Appendix Table 2. Average Random-Weight Cheese Prices by U.S. Region, 1998-2003**

| Product | 1998 | 1999 | 2000 | 2001 | 2002 | 2003 |
|---|---|---|---|---|---|---|
| | *Dollars* | | | | | |
| **American cheese (Pound)** | | | | | | |
| East | 2.73 | 3.57 | 3.40 | 3.68 | 3.81 | 3.83 |
| Midwest | 2.82 | 3.72 | 3.70 | 4.26 | 3.92 | 3.66 |
| South | 3.06 | 3.75 | 3.43 | 3.72 | 3.84 | 3.84 |
| West | 2.81 | 3.44 | 3.82 | 3.49 | 3.73 | 3.96 |
| **Cheddar cheese (Pound)** | | | | | | |
| East | 3.76 | 3.76 | 3.74 | 3.98 | 4.22 | 4.34 |
| Midwest | 3.53 | 3.65 | 3.41 | 3.70 | 3.68 | 3.47 |
| South | 3.83 | 3.09 | 3.23 | 3.38 | 3.46 | 3.39 |
| West | 4.19 | 3.18 | 3.24 | 3.28 | 3.48 | 3.43 |
| **Colby cheese (Pound)** | | | | | | |
| East | 3.31 | 3.37 | 3.82 | 3.93 | 3.77 | 3.48 |
| Midwest | 3.10 | 3.38 | 3.19 | 3.49 | 3.43 | 3.43 |
| South | 3.18 | 3.27 | 2.97 | 3.75 | 3.65 | 3.37 |
| West | 3.60 | 2.95 | 2.90 | 3.03 | 2.94 | 2.72 |
| **Cream cheese (Pound)** | | | | | | |
| East | 4.03 | 5.02 | 3.42 | 3.94 | 3.69 | 3.99 |
| Midwest | 2.26 | 2.77 | 3.06 | 3.77 | 2.67 | 3.43 |
| South | 1.30 | 3.14 | 3.96 | 3.06 | 3.36 | 2.71 |
| West | 1.97 | 3.35 | 3.18 | 3.80 | 2.71 | 4.71 |
| **Mozzarella cheese (Pound)** | | | | | | |
| East | 3.05 | 3.75 | 3.99 | 4.44 | 4.60 | 4.42 |
| Midwest | 3.17 | 3.05 | 2.92 | 3.07 | 3.06 | 3.28 |
| South | 2.79 | 3.08 | 3.09 | 3.86 | 3.36 | 3.54 |
| West | 2.96 | 3.19 | 3.23 | 3.19 | 3.91 | 3.63 |
| **Muenster cheese (Pound)** | | | | | | |
| East | 2.01 | 3.98 | 3.84 | 3.63 | 4.06 | 3.86 |
| Midwest | 1.92 | 3.62 | 3.86 | 4.09 | 3.78 | 3.51 |
| South | 2.41 | 3.98 | 3.46 | 3.77 | 3.47 | 3.62 |
| West | 2.65 | 4.33 | 3.98 | 4.17 | 4.01 | 4.52 |
| **Swiss cheese (Pound)** | | | | | | |
| East | 4.78 | 4.65 | 4.54 | 4.73 | 4.73 | 4.61 |
| Midwest | 4.68 | 4.24 | 4.29 | 4.33 | 4.52 | 4.82 |
| South | 4.60 | 4.69 | 4.34 | 4.76 | 4.89 | 4.74 |
| West | 4.90 | 4.63 | 4.40 | 4.58 | 4.67 | 4.71 |

Source: ERS calculations using ACNielsen Homescan data.

**Appendix Table 3. Average Dairy Prices in Major U.S. Markets, 1998-2003**

| Product | 1998 | 1999 | 2000 | 2001 | 2002 | 2003 |
|---|---|---|---|---|---|---|
| | *Dollars* | | | | | |
| **American cheese (Pound)** | | | | | | |
| Chicago | 2.65 | 2.76 | 2.81 | 2.65 | 2.67 | 2.43 |
| Los Angeles | 3.08 | 3.20 | 3.29 | 3.48 | 3.37 | 3.38 |
| New York | 2.95 | 2.95 | 2.89 | 3.07 | 2.99 | 3.03 |
| San Francisco | 3.37 | 3.29 | 3.63 | 3.82 | 4.03 | 4.33 |
| Atlanta | 2.70 | 2.76 | 2.70 | 2.73 | 2.64 | 2.50 |
| Philadelphia | 2.71 | 2.72 | 2.85 | 2.96 | 2.81 | 2.78 |
| Baltimore-Washington | 2.87 | 3.09 | 3.11 | 3.03 | 2.99 | 2.99 |
| San Antonio | 2.95 | 3.14 | 3.22 | 3.01 | 2.89 | 2.70 |
| Nonmetro | 2.74 | 2.77 | 2.86 | 2.71 | 2.62 | 2.49 |
| **Butter (Pound)** | | | | | | |
| Chicago | 2.61 | 2.33 | 2.16 | 2.71 | 2.44 | 2.20 |
| Los Angeles | 2.62 | 2.48 | 2.32 | 3.00 | 3.27 | 2.77 |
| New York | 2.94 | 2.66 | 2.46 | 3.00 | 2.51 | 2.20 |
| San Francisco | 2.78 | 2.56 | 2.62 | 3.44 | 3.24 | 3.04 |
| Atlanta | 2.85 | 2.62 | 2.33 | 2.79 | 2.29 | 2.14 |
| Philadelphia | 2.59 | 2.30 | 2.10 | 2.63 | 2.16 | 2.06 |
| Baltimore-Washington | 2.71 | 2.45 | 2.22 | 2.84 | 2.21 | 2.09 |
| San Antonio | 2.48 | 2.50 | 2.28 | 2.68 | 2.53 | 2.23 |
| Nonmetro | 2.52 | 2.28 | 2.07 | 2.58 | 2.15 | 2.03 |
| **Cheddar cheese (Pound)** | | | | | | |
| Chicago | 3.27 | 3.61 | 3.26 | 3.24 | 3.40 | 3.46 |
| Los Angeles | 3.98 | 4.10 | 3.73 | 4.27 | 4.11 | 3.85 |
| New York | 3.91 | 3.84 | 3.80 | 3.89 | 3.88 | 3.76 |
| San Francisco | 4.08 | 4.98 | 4.19 | 4.31 | 4.86 | 5.12 |
| Atlanta | 3.40 | 3.54 | 3.24 | 3.51 | 3.59 | 3.44 |
| Philadelphia | 3.43 | 3.76 | 3.65 | 3.73 | 3.61 | 3.71 |
| Baltimore-Washington | 3.68 | 3.92 | 3.82 | 3.83 | 3.71 | 3.83 |
| San Antonio | 3.65 | 3.63 | 3.76 | 3.86 | 3.64 | 3.88 |
| Nonmetro | 3.45 | 3.65 | 3.2 | 3.42 | 3.38 | 3.48 |
| **Colby cheese (Pound)** | | | | | | |
| Chicago | 3.20 | 3.61 | 3.27 | 3.38 | 2.92 | 3.20 |
| Los Angeles | 3.50 | 3.16 | 3.02 | 3.73 | 3.89 | 3.81 |

**Appendix Table 3. (Continued)**

| Product | 1998 | 1999 | 2000 | 2001 | 2002 | 2003 |
|---|---|---|---|---|---|---|
| | *Dollars* | | | | | |
| New York | 3.98 | 4.27 | 3.98 | 3.30 | 2.97 | 3.08 |
| San Francisco | NA | NA | 2.69 | 3.65 | 3.19 | 2.67 |
| Atlanta | 2.82 | 3.16 | 2.78 | 3.14 | 3.08 | 3.15 |
| Philadelphia | 2.89 | 2.93 | 3.79 | 3.27 | 3.09 | 2.94 |
| Baltimore-Washington | 3.51 | 3.19 | 3.17 | 3.43 | 3.52 | 3.23 |
| San Antonio | 3.05 | 3.52 | 3.06 | 3.23 | 3.08 | 3.10 |
| Nonmetro | 3.13 | 3.30 | 3.09 | 3.28 | 3.15 | 3.19 |
| **Cottage cheese (Pound)** | | | | | | |
| Chicago | 1.42 | 1.57 | 1.54 | 1.59 | 1.53 | 1.58 |
| Los Angeles | 1.66 | 1.78 | 1.71 | 1.90 | 1.75 | 1.76 |
| New York | 1.78 | 1.82 | 1.91 | 1.95 | 1.93 | 1.97 |
| San Francisco | 1.90 | 1.92 | 1.87 | 1.84 | 2.04 | 2.13 |
| Atlanta | 1.40 | 1.47 | 1.41 | 1.39 | 1.41 | 1.46 |
| Philadelphia | 1.57 | 1.72 | 1.70 | 1.73 | 1.71 | 1.71 |
| Baltimore-Washington | 1.65 | 1.74 | 1.74 | 1.73 | 1.76 | 1.76 |
| San Antonio | 1.54 | 1.58 | 1.66 | 1.68 | 1.62 | 1.42 |
| Nonmetro | 1.36 | 1.43 | 1.42 | 1.43 | 1.44 | 1.42 |
| **Cream cheese (Pound)** | | | | | | |
| Chicago | 2.33 | 2.55 | 2.42 | 2.64 | 2.55 | 2.60 |
| Los Angeles | 2.59 | 2.86 | 2.83 | 2.96 | 3.06 | 3.18 |
| New York | 2.93 | 2.85 | 2.83 | 2.80 | 2.69 | 2.70 |
| San Francisco | 2.83 | 2.92 | 3.15 | 3.41 | 3.69 | 3.88 |
| Atlanta | 2.48 | 2.52 | 2.47 | 2.57 | 2.50 | 2.39 |
| Philadelphia | 2.36 | 2.39 | 2.41 | 2.54 | 2.39 | 2.37 |
| Baltimore-Washington | 2.49 | 2.65 | 2.54 | 2.66 | 2.54 | 2.58 |
| San Antonio | 2.27 | 2.27 | 2.23 | 2.33 | 2.36 | 2.22 |
| Nonmetro | 2.41 | 2.55 | 2.44 | 2.56 | 2.5 | 2.43 |
| **Extra large eggs (Dozen)** | | | | | | |
| Chicago | 1.10 | 1.00 | 1.00 | 1.07 | 0.93 | 1.13 |
| Los Angeles | 1.21 | 1.30 | 1.33 | 1.21 | 1.25 | 1.37 |
| New York | 1.29 | 1.11 | 1.06 | 1.09 | 1.10 | 1.23 |
| San Francisco | 1.75 | 1.45 | 1.55 | 1.66 | 1.64 | 1.92 |
| Atlanta | 1.01 | 0.94 | 1.08 | 1.17 | 1.29 | 1.41 |
| Philadelphia | 1.07 | 1.13 | 1.08 | 1.06 | 1.08 | 1.19 |

**Appendix Table 3. (Continued)**

| Product | 1998 | 1999 | 2000 | 2001 | 2002 | 2003 |
|---|---|---|---|---|---|---|
| | *Dollars* | | | | | |
| Baltimore-Washington | 1.09 | 0.97 | 1.01 | 0.99 | 1.03 | 1.23 |
| San Antonio | 1.00 | 0.96 | 1.01 | 1.07 | 1.16 | 1.30 |
| Nonmetro | 1.05 | 0.92 | 0.94 | 0.93 | 0.94 | 1.19 |
| **Farmers cheese (Pound)** | | | | | | |
| Chicago | 3.48 | 3.22 | 4.81 | 3.34 | 3.58 | 3.28 |
| Los Angeles | 3.91 | 5.24 | 4.28 | 3.14 | 5.69 | 7.28 |
| New York | 3.38 | 3.52 | 4.29 | 4.06 | 3.86 | 4.19 |
| San Francisco | NA | NA | NA | 6.78 | 5.36 | 4.75 |
| Atlanta | 3.71 | 4.07 | 7.98 | 3.29 | 6.26 | 4.10 |
| Philadelphia | NA | NA | 4.00 | 4.84 | 5.09 | 4.57 |
| Baltimore-Washington | 3.90 | 4.62 | 5.11 | 3.35 | 3.41 | 4.20 |
| San Antonio | 4.48 | 4.58 | NA | 4.47 | 6.31 | 6.73 |
| Nonmetro | 4.99 | 3.05 | 3.28 | 4.48 | 5.77 | 5.11 |
| **Frozen yogurt (Half-Gallon)** | | | | | | |
| Chicago | 4.13 | 4.22 | 3.92 | 4.24 | 5.66 | 5.82 |
| Los Angeles | 4.86 | 5.38 | 5.25 | 7.05 | 6.19 | 9.37 |
| New York | 3.53 | 3.49 | 3.28 | 3.59 | 3.66 | 4.22 |
| San Francisco | 6.92 | 4.90 | 5.26 | 5.84 | 6.79 | 7.97 |
| Atlanta | 2.91 | 3.57 | 3.13 | 3.13 | 3.01 | 2.70 |
| Philadelphia | 3.31 | 3.19 | 3.61 | 3.52 | 3.39 | 3.45 |
| Baltimore-Washington | 3.40 | 3.57 | 3.69 | 3.94 | 3.94 | 4.71 |
| San Antonio | 3.71 | 3.80 | 5.17 | 5.07 | 3.47 | 3.95 |
| Nonmetro | 3.16 | 3.16 | 3.24 | 3.39 | 3.21 | 3.35 |
| **Ice cream (Half-Gallon)** | | | | | | |
| Chicago | 3.00 | 3.03 | 3.16 | 3.23 | 3.57 | 3.36 |
| Los Angeles | 3.76 | 4.02 | 3.97 | 4.08 | 3.99 | 4.26 |
| New York | 3.09 | 3.44 | 3.26 | 3.50 | 3.69 | 3.88 |
| San Francisco | 3.48 | 4.08 | 4.24 | 4.31 | 4.70 | 4.65 |
| Atlanta | 3.11 | 3.28 | 3.14 | 3.44 | 3.26 | 3.13 |
| Philadelphia | 2.74 | 3.02 | 3.00 | 3.02 | 2.96 | 3.00 |
| Baltimore-Washington | 3.11 | 3.34 | 3.27 | 3.36 | 3.51 | 3.54 |
| San Antonio | 3.30 | 3.59 | 3.63 | 3.72 | 3.68 | 3.86 |
| Nonmetro | 2.90 | 3.01 | 2.99 | 3.06 | 3.05 | 3.03 |

**Appendix Table 3. (Continued)**

| Product | 1998 | 1999 | 2000 | 2001 | 2002 | 2003 |
|---|---|---|---|---|---|---|
| | *Dollars* | | | | | |
| **Jumbo eggs (Dozen)** | | | | | | |
| Chicago | 1.20 | 1.25 | 1.29 | 1.35 | 1.25 | 1.48 |
| Los Angeles | 2.11 | 1.65 | 1.49 | 1.62 | 1.43 | 1.79 |
| New York | 1.45 | 1.35 | 1.33 | 1.36 | 1.37 | 1.54 |
| San Francisco | 1.91 | 1.87 | 1.86 | 1.83 | 2.06 | 2.10 |
| Atlanta | 1.12 | 1.01 | 1.09 | 1.13 | 1.07 | 1.28 |
| Philadelphia | 1.23 | 0.93 | 1.09 | 1.22 | 1.26 | 1.35 |
| Baltimore-Washington | 1.23 | 1.09 | 1.13 | 1.10 | 1.14 | 1.29 |
| San Antonio | 1.11 | 1.10 | 0.93 | 1.06 | 1.19 | 1.33 |
| Nonmetro | 1.14 | 0.92 | 1.01 | 1.03 | 1.03 | 1.20 |
| **Large eggs (Dozen)** | | | | | | |
| Chicago | 0.94 | 0.82 | 0.89 | 0.92 | 0.91 | 1.15 |
| Los Angeles | 1.53 | 1.40 | 1.39 | 1.54 | 1.59 | 1.68 |
| New York | 1.35 | 1.27 | 1.30 | 1.37 | 1.35 | 1.56 |
| San Francisco | 1.36 | 1.29 | 1.41 | 1.47 | 1.68 | 2.00 |
| Atlanta | 0.96 | 0.86 | 0.91 | 0.99 | 0.94 | 1.11 |
| Philadelphia | 1.03 | 0.93 | 0.98 | 0.98 | 1.00 | 1.16 |
| Baltimore-Washington | 1.01 | 0.90 | 0.91 | 0.93 | 0.96 | 1.17 |
| San Antonio | 0.99 | 0.95 | 0.93 | 0.97 | 0.94 | 1.08 |
| Nonmetro | 0.94 | 0.86 | 0.85 | 0.90 | 0.91 | 1.09 |
| **Low-fat milk (Gallon)** | | | | | | |
| Chicago | 2.17 | 2.35 | 2.34 | 2.28 | 2.16 | 2.14 |
| Los Angeles | 2.61 | 2.69 | 2.37 | 2.66 | 2.16 | 2.32 |
| New York | 2.46 | 2.61 | 2.52 | 2.58 | 2.49 | 2.50 |
| San Francisco | 2.77 | 2.49 | 2.45 | 2.64 | 2.47 | 2.60 |
| Atlanta | 2.49 | 2.68 | 2.80 | 2.85 | 2.73 | 2.68 |
| Philadelphia | 2.36 | 2.49 | 2.51 | 2.74 | 2.70 | 2.75 |
| Baltimore-Washington | 2.44 | 2.45 | 2.44 | 2.62 | 2.56 | 2.51 |
| San Antonio | 2.28 | 2.41 | 2.61 | 2.77 | 2.59 | 2.74 |
| Nonmetro | 2.32 | 2.48 | 2.48 | 2.51 | 2.40 | 2.38 |
| **Margarine (Pound)** | | | | | | |
| Chicago | 0.85 | 0.85 | 0.87 | 0.93 | 0.78 | 0.83 |
| Los Angeles | 0.88 | 0.96 | 0.94 | 0.97 | 0.97 | 0.99 |
| New York | 1.11 | 0.96 | 0.96 | 0.96 | 0.96 | 1.07 |

**Appendix Table 3. (Continued)**

| Product | 1998 | 1999 | 2000 | 2001 | 2002 | 2003 |
|---|---|---|---|---|---|---|
| | *Dollars* | | | | | |
| San Francisco | 1.12 | 1.00 | 0.97 | 1.11 | 0.99 | 1.09 |
| Atlanta | 0.75 | 0.79 | 0.72 | 0.75 | 0.69 | 0.77 |
| Philadelphia | 0.86 | 0.97 | 0.91 | 0.95 | 0.89 | 0.92 |
| Baltimore-Washington | 0.92 | 0.90 | 0.91 | 0.94 | 0.86 | 0.88 |
| San Antonio | 0.76 | 0.74 | 0.71 | 0.73 | 0.67 | 0.64 |
| Nonmetro | 0.82 | 0.80 | 0.80 | 0.79 | 0.75 | 0.74 |
| **Medium eggs (Dozen)** | | | | | | |
| Chicago | 0.88 | 0.75 | 0.80 | 0.81 | 0.68 | 0.90 |
| Los Angeles | 1.21 | 1.06 | 1.09 | 1.27 | 1.08 | 1.38 |
| New York | 1.25 | 0.83 | 0.86 | 0.93 | 0.93 | 1.10 |
| San Francisco | 1.62 | 1.73 | 1.16 | 1.45 | 1.30 | 1.42 |
| Atlanta | 0.70 | 0.67 | 0.71 | 0.74 | 0.63 | 0.83 |
| Philadelphia | 0.74 | 0.74 | 0.85 | 0.88 | 0.84 | 0.99 |
| Baltimore-Washington | 0.74 | 0.69 | 0.78 | 0.76 | 0.74 | 0.96 |
| San Antonio | 0.79 | 0.75 | 0.78 | 0.87 | 0.78 | 0.90 |
| Nonmetro | 0.69 | 0.63 | 0.66 | 0.70 | 0.68 | 0.89 |
| **Mozzarella cheese (Pound)** | | | | | | |
| Chicago | 3.00 | 3.26 | 3.43 | 3.41 | 3.73 | 3.80 |
| Los Angeles | 4.05 | 4.06 | 3.89 | 4.01 | 4.47 | 4.22 |
| New York | 2.79 | 2.89 | 2.78 | 2.99 | 2.95 | 3.05 |
| San Francisco | 3.61 | 4.07 | 3.76 | 4.49 | 4.65 | 4.92 |
| Atlanta | 3.23 | 3.65 | 3.60 | 3.48 | 3.49 | 3.40 |
| Philadelphia | 2.97 | 2.81 | 3.28 | 3.39 | 3.27 | 3.12 |
| Baltimore-Washington | 3.05 | 3.32 | 3.78 | 3.73 | 3.50 | 3.72 |
| San Antonio | 3.24 | 3.59 | 3.28 | 3.92 | 3.65 | 3.73 |
| Nonmetro | 3.31 | 3.40 | 3.24 | 3.40 | 3.45 | 3.52 |
| **Muenster cheese (Pound)** | | | | | | |
| Chicago | 3.50 | 3.89 | 3.47 | 3.88 | 4.02 | 4.44 |
| Los Angeles | 4.30 | 4.87 | 6.96 | 5.54 | 5.98 | 5.78 |
| New York | 4.01 | 4.26 | 4.24 | 4.56 | 4.94 | 4.79 |
| San Francisco | NA | NA | NA | 7.72 | 5.81 | 5.20 |
| Atlanta | 3.62 | 3.53 | 3.16 | 3.58 | 5.05 | 4.83 |
| Philadelphia | 6.78 | 2.81 | 3.99 | 4.13 | 4.05 | 3.85 |
| Baltimore-Washington | 4.13 | 3.91 | 4.34 | 4.77 | 5.44 | 5.59 |

**Appendix Table 3. (Continued)**

| Product | 1998 | 1999 | 2000 | 2001 | 2002 | 2003 |
|---|---|---|---|---|---|---|
| | *Dollars* | | | | | |
| San Antonio | 6.38 | 6.30 | NA | 4.02 | 4.85 | 5.35 |
| Nonmetro | 3.67 | 3.53 | 3.42 | 3.62 | 4.11 | 4.21 |
| **Ricotta cheese (Pound)** | | | | | | |
| Chicago | 1.77 | 1.91 | 1.95 | 1.99 | 1.99 | 2.02 |
| Los Angeles | 2.15 | 2.17 | 2.08 | 2.33 | 2.35 | 2.29 |
| New York | 1.45 | 1.53 | 1.52 | 1.59 | 1.62 | 1.62 |
| San Francisco | 2.07 | 2.44 | 2.42 | 2.56 | 2.65 | 2.66 |
| Atlanta | 1.61 | 1.65 | 1.66 | 1.70 | 1.68 | 1.68 |
| Philadelphia | 1.47 | 1.53 | 1.58 | 1.65 | 1.66 | 1.60 |
| Baltimore-Washington | 1.70 | 1.63 | 1.82 | 1.86 | 1.80 | 1.88 |
| San Antonio | 2.08 | 2.29 | 2.08 | 2.10 | 2.11 | 1.86 |
| Nonmetro | 1.80 | 1.84 | 1.79 | 1.84 | 1.92 | 1.80 |
| **Sherbet (Half-Gallon)** | | | | | | |
| Chicago | 2.84 | 2.76 | 2.99 | 3.29 | 3.30 | 3.34 |
| Los Angeles | 2.90 | 3.04 | 2.85 | 3.31 | 3.04 | 3.11 |
| New York | 3.02 | 3.10 | 3.46 | 3.08 | 3.07 | 3.23 |
| San Francisco | 2.63 | 2.73 | 3.03 | 3.37 | 3.67 | 3.60 |
| Atlanta | 2.16 | 2.25 | 2.38 | 2.51 | 2.61 | 2.67 |
| Philadelphia | 2.93 | 3.06 | 3.29 | 3.39 | 2.99 | 3.30 |
| Baltimore-Washington | 3.20 | 3.40 | 3.73 | 3.82 | 3.70 | 3.42 |
| San Antonio | 3.24 | 3.89 | 3.43 | 3.82 | 3.81 | 3.74 |
| Nonmetro | 2.53 | 2.51 | 2.57 | 2.68 | 2.75 | 2.76 |
| **Skim milk (Gallon)** | | | | | | |
| Chicago | 2.25 | 2.43 | 2.43 | 2.28 | 2.15 | 2.2 |
| Los Angeles | 2.40 | 2.32 | 2.20 | 2.32 | 1.99 | 1.99 |
| New York | 2.58 | 2.65 | 2.54 | 2.52 | 2.53 | 2.55 |
| San Francisco | 2.22 | 2.24 | 2.13 | 2.35 | 2.15 | 2.22 |
| Atlanta | 2.49 | 2.62 | 2.71 | 2.75 | 2.65 | 2.69 |
| Philadelphia | 2.36 | 2.51 | 2.41 | 2.59 | 2.56 | 2.61 |
| Baltimore-Washington | 2.31 | 2.32 | 2.38 | 2.47 | 2.46 | 2.43 |
| San Antonio | 2.22 | 2.38 | 2.57 | 2.73 | 2.52 | 2.64 |
| Nonmetro | 2.10 | 2.27 | 2.26 | 2.28 | 2.25 | 2.22 |
| **Swiss cheese (Pound)** | | | | | | |
| Chicago | 4.03 | 4.47 | 4.31 | 4.26 | 4.41 | 4.12 |

**Appendix Table 3. (Continued)**

| Product | 1998 | 1999 | 2000 | 2001 | 2002 | 2003 |
|---|---|---|---|---|---|---|
| | *Dollars* | | | | | |
| Los Angeles | 4.14 | 4.17 | 4.44 | 5.01 | 4.58 | 4.83 |
| New York | 4.32 | 4.78 | 4.55 | 4.35 | 4.95 | 5.11 |
| San Francisco | 4.82 | 5.04 | 4.16 | 4.19 | 4.96 | 4.85 |
| Atlanta | 4.12 | 4.27 | 4.08 | 4.19 | 4.80 | 4.34 |
| Philadelphia | 4.03 | 4.63 | 4.23 | 4.17 | 4.00 | 4.72 |
| Baltimore-Washington | 4.04 | 4.16 | 4.08 | 4.12 | 4.40 | 4.49 |
| San Antonio | 4.53 | 4.56 | 3.63 | 4.57 | 4.35 | 4.83 |
| Nonmetro | 4.38 | 4.12 | 4.48 | 4.18 | 4.39 | 4.11 |
| **Whole milk (Gallon)** | | | | | | |
| Chicago | 2.35 | 2.56 | 2.69 | 2.47 | 2.31 | 2.20 |
| Los Angeles | 2.70 | 2.86 | 2.43 | 2.92 | 2.18 | 2.32 |
| New York | 2.53 | 2.77 | 2.69 | 2.70 | 2.61 | 2.68 |
| San Francisco | 2.73 | 2.48 | 2.50 | 2.92 | 2.57 | 2.72 |
| Atlanta | 2.54 | 2.68 | 2.75 | 2.85 | 2.77 | 2.77 |
| Philadelphia | 2.60 | 2.69 | 2.59 | 2.92 | 2.82 | 2.84 |
| Baltimore-Washington | 2.52 | 2.62 | 2.61 | 2.76 | 2.65 | 2.65 |
| San Antonio | 2.29 | 2.45 | 2.66 | 2.86 | 2.68 | 2.79 |
| Nonmetro | 2.48 | 2.56 | 2.58 | 2.67 | 2.58 | 2.60 |
| **Yogurt (6 ounces)** | | | | | | |
| Chicago | 0.51 | 0.49 | 0.50 | 0.51 | 0.54 | 0.52 |
| Los Angeles | 0.47 | 0.47 | 0.50 | 0.51 | 0.52 | 0.52 |
| New York | 0.51 | 0.52 | 0.54 | 0.53 | 0.56 | 0.55 |
| San Francisco | 0.49 | 0.49 | 0.52 | 0.55 | 0.59 | 0.61 |
| Atlanta | 0.47 | 0.46 | 0.47 | 0.46 | 0.50 | 0.47 |
| Philadelphia | 0.47 | 0.46 | 0.48 | 0.50 | 0.51 | 0.50 |
| Baltimore-Washington | 0.49 | 0.49 | 0.49 | 0.49 | 0.54 | 0.54 |
| San Antonio | 0.44 | 0.42 | 0.41 | 0.41 | 0.48 | 0.46 |
| Nonmetro | 0.46 | 0.46 | 0.47 | 0.46 | 0.49 | 0.48 |
| **Yogurt shakes (16 ounces)** | | | | | | |
| Chicago | NA | NA | 2.30 | 2.36 | 2.19 | 2.09 |
| Los Angeles | NA | NA | 2.18 | 2.16 | 1.92 | 2.10 |
| New York | NA | NA | 2.38 | 2.51 | 2.72 | 2.14 |
| San Francisco | NA | NA | 2.35 | 2.53 | 2.67 | 2.53 |
| Atlanta | NA | NA | 2.21 | 2.16 | 2.16 | 2.00 |

**Appendix Table 3. (Continued)**

| Product | 1998 | 1999 | 2000 | 2001 | 2002 | 2003 |
|---|---|---|---|---|---|---|
| | *Dollars* | | | | | |
| Philadelphia | NA | NA | 2.01 | 2.09 | 2.15 | 1.85 |
| Baltimore-Washington | NA | NA | 2.19 | 2.30 | 2.10 | 1.98 |
| San Antonio | NA | NA | 2.02 | 2.28 | 1.70 | 1.84 |
| Nonmetro | NA | NA | 2.20 | 2.15 | 2.16 | 1.94 |

NA = Not available.

Source: ERS calculations using ACNielsen Homescan data.

## Appendix Table 4. Average Random-Weight Cheese Prices in Major U.S. Markets, 1998-2003

| Product | 1998 | 1999 | 2000 | 2001 | 2002 | 2003 |
|---|---|---|---|---|---|---|
| | *Dollars* | | | | | |
| **American cheese (Pound)** | | | | | | |
| Chicago | 2.90 | 4.38 | 3.37 | 5.06 | 4.40 | 4.19 |
| Los Angeles | 2.85 | 3.93 | 4.24 | 3.15 | 3.65 | 3.98 |
| New York | 2.86 | 3.89 | 3.71 | 4.03 | 3.88 | 4.23 |
| San Francisco | NA | NA | 4.56 | 4.07 | 4.41 | 4.74 |
| Atlanta | 2.80 | 4.08 | 4.18 | 3.88 | 4.43 | 4.39 |
| Philadelphia | 2.90 | 3.33 | 3.30 | 3.63 | 3.71 | 3.76 |
| Baltimore-Washington | 2.87 | 3.78 | 3.61 | 3.76 | 4.09 | 4.36 |
| San Antonio | 2.71 | 3.33 | 2.73 | 2.68 | 3.59 | 2.98 |
| Nonmetro | 2.80 | 3.10 | 3.38 | 3.83 | 4.08 | 3.97 |
| **Cheddar cheese (Pound)** | | | | | | |
| Chicago | 3.09 | 4.31 | 4.14 | 3.65 | 4.00 | 3.45 |
| Los Angeles | 4.20 | 3.23 | 3.31 | 3.37 | 4.00 | 3.61 |
| New York | 4.16 | 3.79 | 3.74 | 4.20 | 4.19 | 3.95 |
| San Francisco | 4.06 | 3.97 | 3.69 | 3.98 | 3.93 | 4.09 |
| Atlanta | 3.96 | 3.28 | 3.13 | 3.25 | 3.27 | 3.58 |
| Philadelphia | 2.86 | 3.77 | 3.83 | 3.89 | 4.07 | 4.18 |
| Baltimore-Washington | 3.44 | 3.43 | 3.69 | 3.79 | 4.16 | 4.41 |
| San Antonio | 3.70 | 3.27 | 3.00 | 3.57 | 3.70 | 3.83 |
| Nonmetro | 3.98 | 3.32 | 3.25 | 3.47 | 3.48 | 3.39 |
| **Colby cheese (Pound)** | | | | | | |
| Chicago | 2.81 | 3.73 | 3.66 | 3.61 | 4.16 | 3.82 |
| Los Angeles | 3.13 | 3.33 | 3.56 | 3.18 | 3.28 | 3.55 |
| New York | 4.97 | 4.34 | 5.10 | 4.35 | 4.06 | 4.53 |
| San Francisco | 4.06 | 3.05 | 1.78 | 3.38 | 3.44 | 2.80 |

**Appendix Table 4. (Continued)**

| Product | 1998 | 1999 | 2000 | 2001 | 2002 | 2003 |
|---|---|---|---|---|---|---|
| | *Dollars* | | | | | |
| Atlanta | 3.19 | 3.66 | 3.26 | 3.63 | 3.85 | 3.36 |
| Philadelphia | 3.98 | 3.57 | 3.58 | 3.50 | 2.91 | 3.70 |
| Baltimore-Washington | 2.89 | 3.48 | 3.16 | 3.07 | 3.94 | 3.77 |
| San Antonio | 3.29 | 2.86 | 2.56 | 2.90 | 3.28 | 3.65 |
| Nonmetro | 2.93 | 3.12 | 2.86 | 3.37 | 3.29 | 3.30 |
| **Cream cheese (Pound)** | | | | | | |
| Chicago | 2.35 | 3.57 | 3.49 | 3.05 | 2.96 | 3.23 |
| Los Angeles | 2.37 | 3.21 | 3.28 | 3.99 | 5.01 | 4.96 |
| New York | 4.08 | 5.22 | 4.22 | 4.26 | 4.43 | 4.35 |
| San Francisco | 8.33 | 3.52 | 2.60 | 3.19 | 3.53 | 4.29 |
| Atlanta | 1.85 | 1.81 | NA | NA | NA | NA |
| Philadelphia | NA | NA | NA | NA | NA | NA |
| Baltimore-Washington | NA | 4.02 | 4.72 | 3.91 | 3.74 | 3.29 |
| San Antonio | NA | 3.42 | 3.58 | 3.02 | 2.79 | 4.65 |
| Nonmetro | 1.88 | 2.95 | 3.30 | 3.34 | 2.26 | 3.97 |
| **Mozzarella cheese (Pound)** | | | | | | |
| Chicago | 2.57 | 3.52 | 2.99 | 2.96 | 2.99 | 3.24 |
| Los Angeles | 3.12 | 3.71 | 3.71 | 3.63 | 3.84 | 3.50 |
| New York | 3.07 | 4.25 | 5.02 | 4.83 | 5.10 | 4.83 |
| San Francisco | 2.83 | 4.06 | 3.55 | 3.81 | 4.04 | 4.28 |
| Atlanta | 3.03 | 3.61 | 3.48 | 3.82 | 3.25 | 4.13 |
| Philadelphia | 2.97 | 2.67 | 3.81 | 4.50 | 3.81 | 3.42 |
| Baltimore-Washington | 2.87 | 3.25 | 3.22 | 3.67 | 4.08 | 4.07 |
| San Antonio | 2.86 | 2.75 | 3.66 | 3.97 | 4.26 | 3.43 |
| Nonmetro | 2.67 | 2.97 | 2.96 | 3.13 | 3.09 | 3.29 |
| **Muenster cheese (Pound)** | | | | | | |
| Chicago | 1.58 | 4.25 | 4.31 | 4.70 | 3.64 | 3.63 |
| Los Angeles | 2.70 | 3.52 | 4.55 | 3.62 | 3.89 | 4.40 |
| New York | 2.56 | 4.05 | 3.91 | 3.79 | 4.30 | 4.19 |
| San Francisco | 3.76 | 1.60 | 4.54 | 4.66 | 4.27 | 3.94 |
| Atlanta | 1.65 | 4.13 | 3.66 | 3.96 | 4.60 | 4.20 |
| Philadelphia | 1.61 | 3.56 | 3.60 | 3.59 | 3.79 | 3.61 |
| Baltimore-Washington | 1.96 | 3.81 | 3.99 | 4.16 | 4.51 | 4.62 |
| San Antonio | 2.52 | 3.88 | 3.78 | 4.13 | 3.75 | 3.86 |
| Nonmetro | 2.13 | 3.77 | 3.72 | 3.01 | 3.37 | 3.54 |
| **Swiss cheese (Pound)** | | | | | | |
| Chicago | 4.88 | 4.66 | 4.60 | 5.02 | 4.73 | 4.60 |
| Los Angeles | 4.98 | 4.14 | 5.08 | 4.53 | 4.90 | 5.15 |

**Appendix Table 4. (Continued)**

| Product | 1998 | 1999 | 2000 | 2001 | 2002 | 2003 |
|---|---|---|---|---|---|---|
| | *Dollars* | | | | | |
| New York | 5.02 | 4.70 | 4.51 | 4.75 | 4.58 | 4.90 |
| San Francisco | 4.95 | 5.04 | 3.33 | 4.94 | 5.45 | 5.30 |
| Atlanta | 5.26 | 4.79 | 4.63 | 5.20 | 5.47 | 5.04 |
| Philadelphia | 4.20 | 4.37 | 4.64 | 4.75 | 4.84 | 4.93 |
| Baltimore-Washington | 4.29 | 4.62 | 4.49 | 4.62 | 5.02 | 5.21 |
| San Antonio | 4.77 | 4.67 | 4.44 | 4.64 | 4.45 | 4.46 |
| Nonmetro | 4.95 | 4.52 | 4.15 | 4.59 | 4.56 | 4.74 |

NA = Not available.

Source: ERS calculations using ACNielsen Homescan data.

**Appendix Table 5. Average Dairy Prices by Income Group, 1998-2003**

| Product | 1998 | 1999 | 2000 | 2001 | 2002 | 2003 |
|---|---|---|---|---|---|---|
| | *Dollars* | | | | | |
| **American cheese (Pound)** | | | | | | |
| Income < $25,000 | 2.64 | 2.83 | 2.67 | 2.74 | 2.66 | 2.60 |
| $25,000-$49,999 | 2.72 | 2.84 | 2.86 | 2.81 | 2.70 | 2.55 |
| $50,000-$69,999 | 2.76 | 2.89 | 2.85 | 2.82 | 2.81 | 2.76 |
| Income > $70,000 | 2.98 | 3.01 | 2.97 | 3.07 | 2.93 | 2.94 |
| **Butter (Pound)** | | | | | | |
| Income < 25,000 | 2.56 | 2.44 | 2.13 | 2.64 | 2.16 | 2.02 |
| $25,000-$49,999 | 2.60 | 2.32 | 2.14 | 2.67 | 2.21 | 2.07 |
| $50,000-$69,999 | 2.60 | 2.41 | 2.23 | 2.69 | 2.27 | 2.13 |
| Income > $70,000 | 2.78 | 2.47 | 2.30 | 2.84 | 2.45 | 2.30 |
| **Cheddar cheese (Pound)** | | | | | | |
| Income < 25,000 | 3.46 | 3.60 | 3.11 | 3.44 | 3.46 | 3.57 |
| $25,000-$49,999 | 3.63 | 3.71 | 3.54 | 3.54 | 3.53 | 3.52 |
| $50,000-$69,999 | 3.43 | 3.75 | 3.50 | 3.61 | 3.57 | 3.65 |
| Income > $70,000 | 3.84 | 4.06 | 3.80 | 3.84 | 3.80 | 3.90 |
| **Colby cheese (Pound)** | | | | | | |
| Income < 25,000 | 3.37 | 3.11 | 3.10 | 3.51 | 3.20 | 3.30 |
| $25,000-$49,999 | 2.98 | 3.37 | 3.22 | 3.24 | 3.40 | 3.12 |
| $50,000-$69,999 | 3.11 | 3.27 | 2.98 | 2.96 | 2.92 | 3.29 |
| Income > $70,000 | 3.22 | 3.59 | 3.21 | 3.46 | 3.52 | 3.19 |

**Appendix Table 5. (Continued)**

| Product | 1998 | 1999 | 2000 | 2001 | 2002 | 2003 |
|---|---|---|---|---|---|---|
| | *Dollars* | | | | | |
| **Cottage cheese (Pound)** | | | | | | |
| Income < 25,000 | 1.40 | 1.47 | 1.49 | 1.54 | 1.48 | 1.47 |
| $25,000-$49,999 | 1.43 | 1.50 | 1.49 | 1.50 | 1.54 | 1.49 |
| $50,000-$69,999 | 1.43 | 1.51 | 1.52 | 1.53 | 1.51 | 1.48 |
| Income > $70,000 | 1.48 | 1.55 | 1.59 | 1.61 | 1.62 | 1.58 |
| **Cream cheese (Pound)** | | | | | | |
| Income < 25,000 | 2.45 | 2.62 | 2.48 | 2.55 | 2.46 | 2.48 |
| $25,000-$49,999 | 2.41 | 2.53 | 2.45 | 2.52 | 2.52 | 2.47 |
| $50,000-$69,999 | 2.42 | 2.60 | 2.49 | 2.59 | 2.50 | 2.48 |
| Income > $70,000 | 2.63 | 2.72 | 2.66 | 2.72 | 2.66 | 2.66 |
| **Extra large eggs (Dozen)** | | | | | | |
| Income < 25,000 | 1.11 | 1.01 | 0.94 | 0.98 | 1.00 | 1.20 |
| $25,000-$49,999 | 1.06 | 0.97 | 0.99 | 1.01 | 1.03 | 1.20 |
| $50,000-$69,999 | 1.08 | 0.99 | 0.99 | 0.99 | 1.00 | 1.22 |
| Income > $70,000 | 1.18 | 1.09 | 1.09 | 1.14 | 1.11 | 1.28 |
| **Farmers cheese (Pound)** | | | | | | |
| Income < 25,000 | 3.53 | 3.38 | 4.35 | 3.93 | 3.84 | 4.25 |
| $25,000-$49,999 | 4.93 | 4.83 | 3.67 | 3.95 | 4.09 | 5.14 |
| $50,000-$69,999 | 4.54 | 3.99 | 4.37 | 3.79 | 4.16 | 5.11 |
| Income > $70,000 | 3.68 | 3.15 | 3.79 | 3.89 | 4.77 | 5.39 |
| **Frozen yogurt (Half-Gallon)** | | | | | | |
| Income < 25,000 | 3.16 | 3.95 | 3.13 | 3.44 | 3.38 | 3.15 |
| $25,000-$49,999 | 3.41 | 3.41 | 3.26 | 3.57 | 3.44 | 3.16 |
| $50,000-$69,999 | 3.09 | 3.34 | 3.37 | 3.51 | 3.16 | 3.32 |
| Income > $70,000 | 3.38 | 3.43 | 4.06 | 4.08 | 4.87 | 4.32 |
| **Ice cream (Half-Gallon)** | | | | | | |
| Income < 25,000 | 3.02 | 3.02 | 3.02 | 3.25 | 3.09 | 3.23 |
| $25,000-$49,999 | 2.99 | 3.15 | 3.10 | 3.24 | 3.26 | 3.14 |
| $50,000-$69,999 | 3.08 | 3.25 | 3.17 | 3.34 | 3.32 | 3.16 |
| Income > $70,000 | 3.35 | 3.41 | 3.54 | 3.60 | 3.67 | 3.62 |
| **Jumbo eggs (Dozen)** | | | | | | |
| Income < 25,000 | 1.18 | 1.10 | 1.07 | 1.14 | 1.17 | 1.35 |
| $25,000-$49,999 | 1.18 | 1.01 | 1.07 | 1.13 | 1.10 | 1.27 |
| $50,000-$69,999 | 1.24 | 1.11 | 1.10 | 1.07 | 1.08 | 1.32 |

**Appendix Table 5. (Continued)**

| Product | 1998 | 1999 | 2000 | 2001 | 2002 | 2003 |
|---|---|---|---|---|---|---|
| | *Dollars* | | | | | |
| Income > $70,000 | 1.32 | 1.26 | 1.24 | 1.22 | 1.14 | 1.46 |
| **Large eggs (Dozen)** | | | | | | |
| Income < 25,000 | 0.98 | 0.90 | 0.90 | 0.92 | 0.92 | 1.10 |
| $25,000-$49,999 | 1.00 | 0.90 | 0.92 | 0.95 | 0.96 | 1.14 |
| $50,000-$69,999 | 1.00 | 0.92 | 0.92 | 0.95 | 0.99 | 1.17 |
| Income > $70,000 | 1.1 | 0.98 | 1.04 | 1.06 | 1.07 | 1.29 |
| **Low-fat milk (Gallon)** | | | | | | |
| Income < 25,000 | 2.34 | 2.46 | 2.41 | 2.43 | 2.33 | 2.34 |
| $25,000-$49,999 | 2.30 | 2.48 | 2.41 | 2.50 | 2.34 | 2.38 |
| $50,000-$69,999 | 2.32 | 2.47 | 2.41 | 2.52 | 2.35 | 2.36 |
| Income > $70,000 | 2.36 | 2.54 | 2.44 | 2.54 | 2.40 | 2.40 |
| **Margarine (Pound)** | | | | | | |
| Income < 25,000 | 0.79 | 0.78 | 0.76 | 0.75 | 0.70 | 0.74 |
| $25,000-$49,999 | 0.82 | 0.84 | 0.83 | 0.83 | 0.79 | 0.80 |
| $50,000-$69,999 | 0.87 | 0.87 | 0.87 | 0.90 | 0.84 | 0.86 |
| Income > $70,000 | 0.92 | 0.92 | 0.95 | 0.98 | 0.89 | 0.94 |
| **Medium eggs (Dozen)** | | | | | | |
| Income < 25,000 | 0.77 | 0.70 | 0.73 | 0.77 | 0.70 | 0.94 |
| $25,000-$49,999 | 0.77 | 0.68 | 0.68 | 0.78 | 0.72 | 0.91 |
| $50,000-$69,999 | 0.72 | 0.65 | 0.75 | 0.73 | 0.71 | 0.97 |
| Income > $70,000 | 0.80 | 0.75 | 0.79 | 0.84 | 0.75 | 0.95 |
| **Mozzarella cheese (Pound)** | | | | | | |
| Income < 25,000 | 3.08 | 3.23 | 3.33 | 3.31 | 3.27 | 3.34 |
| $25,000-$49,999 | 3.16 | 3.22 | 3.23 | 3.26 | 3.50 | 3.39 |
| $50,000-$69,999 | 3.19 | 3.19 | 3.36 | 3.44 | 3.62 | 3.59 |
| Income > $70,000 | 3.33 | 3.48 | 3.27 | 3.38 | 3.61 | 3.56 |
| **Muenster cheese (Pound)** | | | | | | |
| Income < 25,000 | 3.40 | 3.98 | 3.09 | 3.43 | 4.14 | 4.48 |
| $25,000-$49,999 | 3.72 | 3.83 | 3.65 | 4.09 | 4.80 | 4.58 |
| $50,000-$69,999 | 3.55 | 3.89 | 3.36 | 4.00 | 5.43 | 4.73 |
| Income > $70,000 | 3.81 | 3.70 | 3.99 | 4.36 | 4.85 | 5.48 |
| **Ricotta cheese (Pound)** | | | | | | |
| Income < 25,000 | 1.67 | 1.75 | 1.67 | 1.85 | 1.85 | 1.71 |
| $25,000-$49,999 | 1.66 | 1.71 | 1.74 | 1.75 | 1.72 | 1.71 |

**Appendix Table 5. (Continued)**

| Product | 1998 | 1999 | 2000 | 2001 | 2002 | 2003 |
|---|---|---|---|---|---|---|
| | *Dollars* | | | | | |
| $50,000-$69,999 | 1.58 | 1.65 | 1.87 | 1.73 | 1.77 | 1.81 |
| Income > $70,000 | 1.67 | 1.70 | 1.63 | 1.73 | 1.79 | 1.80 |
| **Sherbet (Half-Gallon)** | | | | | | |
| Income < 25,000 | 2.77 | 2.73 | 2.79 | 2.71 | 2.80 | 2.91 |
| $25,000-$49,999 | 2.62 | 2.56 | 2.77 | 2.79 | 2.72 | 2.83 |
| $50,000-$69,999 | 2.49 | 2.93 | 2.74 | 3.00 | 3.12 | 2.97 |
| Income > $70,000 | 2.76 | 3.01 | 2.86 | 2.88 | 3.23 | 3.00 |
| **Skim milk (Gallon)** | | | | | | |
| Income < 25,000 | 2.25 | 2.46 | 2.42 | 2.39 | 2.28 | 2.23 |
| $25,000-$49,999 | 2.25 | 2.37 | 2.35 | 2.38 | 2.29 | 2.29 |
| $50,000-$69,999 | 2.21 | 2.39 | 2.36 | 2.38 | 2.25 | 2.21 |
| Income > $70,000 | 2.28 | 2.37 | 2.35 | 2.38 | 2.27 | 2.26 |
| **Swiss cheese (Pound)** | | | | | | |
| Income < 25,000 | 4.21 | 4.04 | 4.29 | 4.24 | 4.47 | 4.30 |
| $25,000-$49,999 | 4.36 | 4.27 | 4.20 | 4.16 | 4.42 | 4.39 |
| $50,000-$69,999 | 4.30 | 4.12 | 4.31 | 4.19 | 4.28 | 4.25 |
| Income > $70,000 | 4.20 | 4.12 | 4.07 | 4.40 | 4.64 | 4.28 |
| **Whole milk (Gallon)** | | | | | | |
| Income < 25,000 | 2.59 | 2.69 | 2.64 | 2.70 | 2.49 | 2.59 |
| $25,000-$49,999 | 2.49 | 2.66 | 2.58 | 2.73 | 2.60 | 2.59 |
| $50,000-$69,999 | 2.53 | 2.66 | 2.64 | 2.73 | 2.64 | 2.63 |
| Income > $70,000 | 2.48 | 2.63 | 2.53 | 2.77 | 2.55 | 2.61 |
| **Yogurt (6 ounces)** | | | | | | |
| Income < 25,000 | 0.44 | 0.44 | 0.46 | 0.46 | 0.47 | 0.48 |
| $25,000-$49,999 | 0.47 | 0.46 | 0.46 | 0.48 | 0.49 | 0.47 |
| $50,000-$69,999 | 0.46 | 0.47 | 0.48 | 0.49 | 0.52 | 0.50 |
| Income > $70,000 | 0.50 | 0.50 | 0.51 | 0.52 | 0.54 | 0.52 |
| **Yogurt shakes (16 ounces)** | | | | | | |
| Income < 25,000 | NA | 2.18 | 2.17 | 1.78 | 2.02 | 1.78 |
| $25,000-$49,999 | NA | 2.66 | 2.20 | 2.22 | 2.18 | 1.89 |
| $50,000-$69,999 | NA | 2.83 | 2.14 | 2.28 | 2.09 | 2.01 |
| Income > $70,000 | NA | 2.55 | 2.35 | 2.16 | 2.29 | 2.04 |

NA = Not available.

Source: ERS calculations using ACNielsen Homescan data.

**Appendix Table 6. Average Random-Weight Cheese Prices by Income Group, 1998-2003**

| Product | 1998 | 1999 | 2000 | 2001 | 2002 | 2003 |
|---|---|---|---|---|---|---|
| | *Dollars* | | | | | |
| **American cheese (Pound)** | | | | | | |
| Income <$25,000 | 2.99 | 3.32 | 3.15 | 3.41 | 3.49 | 3.43 |
| $25,000-$49,999 | 2.88 | 3.57 | 3.37 | 3.46 | 3.85 | 3.90 |
| $50,000-$69,999 | 2.59 | 3.62 | 3.77 | 3.94 | 3.84 | 3.83 |
| Income > $70,000 | 2.86 | 3.97 | 3.61 | 3.95 | 3.92 | 4.08 |
| **Cheddar cheese (Pound)** | | | | | | |
| Income <$25,000 | 3.70 | 3.30 | 3.15 | 3.29 | 3.33 | 3.19 |
| $25,000-$49,999 | 3.95 | 3.23 | 3.34 | 3.34 | 3.47 | 3.61 |
| $50,000-$69,999 | 4.05 | 3.36 | 3.36 | 3.40 | 3.74 | 3.51 |
| Income > $70,000 | 3.91 | 3.52 | 3.60 | 3.96 | 3.98 | 4.03 |
| **Colby cheese (Pound)** | | | | | | |
| Income <$25,000 | 3.15 | 3.12 | 2.71 | 3.08 | 3.08 | 2.90 |
| $25,000-$49,999 | 3.24 | 3.06 | 3.30 | 3.54 | 3.26 | 3.38 |
| $50,000-$69,999 | 3.32 | 3.53 | 3.31 | 3.58 | 3.58 | 3.15 |
| Income > $70,000 | 3.15 | 3.65 | 3.27 | 3.89 | 3.69 | 3.60 |
| **Cream cheese (Pound)** | | | | | | |
| Income <$25,000 | 3.89 | 4.29 | 2.71 | 3.50 | 3.20 | 3.30 |
| $25,000-$49,999 | 2.00 | 3.08 | 3.41 | 3.53 | 3.33 | 3.38 |
| $50,000-$69,999 | 1.82 | 3.62 | 4.07 | 3.77 | 2.32 | 3.60 |
| Income > $70,000 | 1.93 | 4.02 | 3.65 | 4.05 | 3.74 | 5.11 |
| **Mozzarella cheese (Pound)** | | | | | | |
| Income <$25,000 | 2.90 | 2.94 | 2.94 | 3.43 | 3.08 | 3.26 |
| $25,000-$49,999 | 2.93 | 3.33 | 3.26 | 3.39 | 3.52 | 3.92 |
| $50,000-$69,999 | 3.20 | 3.04 | 3.42 | 3.91 | 4.00 | 3.87 |
| Income > $70,000 | 3.19 | 4.03 | 3.48 | 3.91 | 4.40 | 4.07 |
| **Muenster cheese (Pound)** | | | | | | |
| Income <$25,000 | 2.58 | 4.02 | 3.82 | 3.57 | 3.59 | 3.61 |
| $25,000-$49,999 | 2.29 | 3.94 | 3.98 | 3.65 | 3.69 | 3.65 |
| $50,000-$69,999 | 1.72 | 3.71 | 3.34 | 4.01 | 4.12 | 3.87 |
| Income > $70,000 | 1.96 | 3.99 | 3.84 | 4.08 | 3.76 | 3.86 |
| **Swiss cheese (Pound)** | | | | | | |
| Income <$25,000 | 4.48 | 4.42 | 3.83 | 4.07 | 4.27 | 4.27 |
| $25,000-$49,999 | 4.78 | 4.43 | 4.49 | 4.72 | 4.65 | 4.62 |
| $50,000-$69,999 | 4.57 | 4.69 | 4.69 | 4.71 | 4.76 | 4.45 |
| Income > $70,000 | 5.09 | 4.74 | 4.77 | 4.87 | 4.99 | 5.22 |

Source: ERS calculations using ACNielsen Homescan data.

## End Notes

[1] A December 2003 study by UBS Investment Research found a price gap of 17.3 percent to 26.2 percent. The previous year UBS found a price gap of 20.8 percent to 39.1 percent. For a specified identical market basket, UBS found Wal-Mart supercenters to have an average price 19.1 percent lower in Tampa and 22.8 percent lower in Las Vegas.

[2] When customers shift from conventional supermarkets to nontraditional retailers, no change occurs in the food CPI. To the extent that prices at these outlets decrease (or increase) at a different rate than conventional stores, the food CPI will take account of this change with a lagged effect over time.

[3] If only UPC-coded products were used to measure food-at-home expenditures, many food purchases would not be recorded in the data and food-at-home expenditure shares by store type would not accurately measure true household and market expenditure shares. This is especially true when nontraditional stores sell fewer random-weight items than traditional retailers. Leaving out random-weight items would then tend to overstate the shares of food expenditures captured by nontraditional retail outlets.

[4] In total, there were over 17,000 unique households in the data with some subset participating each year creating a total of 48,005 householdby-year observations. In 1998, there were 7,624 households, 7,124 households in 1999, 7,523 in 2000, 8,216 in 2001, 8,685 in 2002, and 8,833 in 2003. Some households participated in the panel for more than 1 year with 35 percent participating in only 1 year, 19 percent participating for 2 years, 14 percent for 3 years, 10 percent for 4 years, 9 percent for 5 years, and 13 percent for all 6 years.

[5] Households lost through attrition are replaced with others having similar key characteristics.

[6] Age, gender, education, occupation of head(s) of household, number of household members, household income, household composition, race, and ethnicity.

[7] Grocery, drug, mass merchandiser, supercenter, club, convenience, other (including dollar stores, bakeries, military stores, online purchases, health food stores, and vending machines).

[8] Dry grocery, dairy, frozen-producemeat, random weight.

[9] The ACNielsen store-level sample is updated through both replacement of canceled or closed stores and a Continuous Sample Improvement Program, whereby the sample is changed intentionally to ensure that changes in the universe are reflected in the sample.

[10] Annual average price variation was calculated by taking the weighted average in a given year and calculating the percentage change with respect to the weighted average of the previous year.

[11] The skim milk category includes all gallon containers of milk purchased with a UPC description that includes some fat-free, no-fat, or skim label. The low-fat milk category includes all gallon containers of milk purchased with a UPC description that includes low fat, 1/2%, 1%, or 2%. The whole-milk category includes all gallon containers of milk with a UPC description that includes “whole” in the descrip-

[12] Average prices across region, income, and market are presented in the appendix.

[13] Atlanta, Baltimore/Washington, Chicago, Los Angeles, New York, Philadelphia, San Antonio, and San Francisco.

[14] Midwest prices were 8.4 percent below East prices, while West prices were 8.2 percent above East prices.

[15] In the ACNielsen Homescan data, nonmetro consumers are defined as any household not living in the top 50 U.S. markets and comprise approximately 15 percent of the sample each year.

[16] At the 5-percent level.

# INDEX

## A



## B

## E



## F

## M



## N



## O



## P

## R



## S

## T



## U